Music Discourse from Classical to Early Modern Times:

Editing and Translating Texts

Music Discourse from Classical to Early Modern Times:
Editing and Translating Texts

Papers given at the
Twenty-Sixth Annual Conference
on Editorial Problems
University of Toronto,
19–20 October 1990

Edited by Maria Rika Maniates

UNIVERSITY OF TORONTO PRESS
Toronto   Buffalo   London

ISBN 0-8020-0972-7

Printed on acid-free paper

Canadian Cataloguing in Publication Data

Conference on Editorial Problems (26th : 1990 : University
of Toronto)
Music discourse from classical to early modern times :
editing and translating texts : papers given at the Twenty-
sixth Annual Conference on Editorial Problems, University of
Toronto, 19–20 October 1990

ISBN 0-8020-0972-7

1. Musicology – Congresses.   2. Editing – Congresses.
3. Music – History and criticism – Early works to 1800 –
Translating – Congresses.   4. Music – Theory – Early works
to 1800 – Translating – Congresses.   I. Maniates, Maria
Rika, 1937–   . II. Title.

ML3797.C65 1990   418′.02   C97-930481-4

University of Toronto Press acknowledges the
financial assistance to its publishing program of the
Canada Council and the Ontario Arts Council

Contents

Members of the Conference

Bo Alphonse *University of Montreal*
Mark Anson-Cartwright *University of Toronto*
Gerald E. Bentley, Jr. *University of Toronto*
Alan C. Bowen **Speaker** *Institute for Research in Classical Philosophy and Science (Princeton)*
William R. Bowen **Speaker** *University of Toronto*
Durrell Bowman *University of Toronto*
Terry Brown *University of Toronto*
Stephanie Conn *University of Toronto*
Stillman Drake **Chair** *University of Toronto*
Maureen Epp *University of Toronto*
Michelle Garon *University of Toronto*
Bryan Gillingham *Carleton University*
John Grant *University of Toronto*
Rebecca Green *University of Toronto*
James Grier **Speaker** *Yale University*
Jennifer Griesbach *University of Toronto*
Andrew Hughes **Chair** *University of Toronto*
Paul Jessen *University of Montreal*
Herta Kreyszig *University of Ottawa*
Walter K. Kreyszig **Speaker** *University of Saskatchewan*
John Lennox *York University*
Maria Rika Maniates **Convenor/Chair** *University of Toronto*
Kurt Markstrom *University of Toronto*
Bryan Martin *University of Toronto*
Suzanne Meyers Sawa *University of Toronto*
Claude V. Palisca **Speaker** *Yale University*
Janet Paterson *University of Toronto*
Pamela L. Poulin *SUNY at Cortland*
Brian E. Power *University of Toronto*
Jay Rahn *York University*
Aubrey Rosenberg *University of Toronto*
George Dimitri Sawa **Speaker** *University of Toronto*
Germaine Warkentin *University of Toronto*

Introduction

The twenty-sixth Conference on Editorial Problems is the first on music. The theme of the conference concerns problems in editing and translating discourse about music—that is, writings on music theory, composition, philosophy, harmonic science, sociology, liturgy, and performance practice. Thus, though the subject matter is music, the material under scrutiny is connected to many cognate disciplines.

The conference is multidisciplinary not only with respect to cognate fields of inquiry, but also with respect to the study of music itself, for it embraces musicology and ethnomusicology, historical and systematic research, philology and hermeneutics. And yet, a common thread can be discerned in the continuity of the history of ideas, indeed of the very idea of music, through the time-span covered by the subject matter. The legacy of the ancient classics, both in general and in particular, remains a stable element in music discourse up to early modern times, no matter how differently that legacy might be interpreted from time to time.

The keynote speaker, Claude V. Palisca, is a senior and highly respected specialist in the field. The thrust of Palisca's paper reflects his wide experience in dealing with sources from classical times through the seventeenth century. He discusses problems of translation: how does one render the original syntax, imagery, style, and vocabulary, both technical and otherwise. In addition to a survey of the issues, Palisca provides samples in Latin and Italian, ranging from the medieval theorist and teacher, Guido of Arezzo, to such renaissance and early modern theorists and critics as Johannes Tinctoris, Nicola Vicentino, Gioseffo Zarlino, and Giovanni Bardi.

Two papers on medieval topics connect music to the ideational world and the practical world. George Dimitri Sawa, an ethnomusicologist fluent in Arabic, deals with editing and translating the myriad Arabic-Persian sources (ranging from speculative philosophy to amusing anecdote) in which are found descriptions of music: its theory, performance, instruments, pedagogy, personalities, social status, intellectual relevance, and the like. Equally intriguing are the problems Sawa shares with scholars of western European sources and the problems exclusive to his work; for instance, how Arabic words should be presented in a modern edition.

Language, in another sense and context, emerges as a central issue in James Grier's paper on the medieval Propers for the Abbey of Saint Martial, rewritten by Adémar de Chabannes to create an apostolic liturgy for the abbey's patron saint. Grier discusses the problems of relating the rewritten texts to the preexisting texts for Saint Martial, to the recognized canonical Propers, and to the polemic about the apostolicity of the saint himself. The thrust of his paper is that, the study of the transmission of the chants aside, a knowledge of ecclesiology, liturgics, and philology must be brought to bear on the editing of this material.

Two speakers, Alan C. Bowen and William R. Bowen, are brothers who share an interest in classical music theory, especially harmonic science, and its survival in medieval and renaissance thought. Alan Bowen is a philosopher who specializes in ancient Greek philosophy and knows music theory; William Bowen is a musicologist who specializes in renaissance music theory and knows philosophy. When asked to prepare a paper as a team, they came up with an unusual topic: how the reception of a text can affect its form when the archetype has been lost. Taking Boethius as their exemplar of the translator as interpreter, they discuss two ancient Greek treatises that survive in Latin versions: Ptolemy's *Harmonica*, and Euclid's *Sectio canonis,* a work whose rightful place in the Euclidian canon is doubted by some, but not by the Bowens.

Though Walter K. Kreyszig's paper approaches the subject of reception from another perspective, it is related to the Bowen essay. Kreyszig discusses the problems of preparing humanist texts for a modern readership. Since Franchino Gaffurio was a learned music theorist, his *Theorica musice* can be taken as representing the standards of the antiquarian community in the renaissance. Gaffurio wrote in Latin, and read both ancient and medieval sources in Latin. Thus, many linguistic layers are evident in the text, and some of these have colored the sources cited in it. Kreyszig examines the issues specific to his text, as well as the current state of musicological expertise in editing and translating treatises in music theory.

At the conference, the papers were divided into three sessions, each chaired by one person who introduced the speakers and coordinated the discussion. The role of the chairs is extremely important, and I wish to thank Stillman Drake and Andrew Hughes for joining me in this function. Outside the formal sessions, the participants were able to exchange information and ideas in a relaxed, informal atmosphere. Conferences on music would be incomplete without live music in concert: in this case, a recital of traditional Arabic music presented by George Dimitri Sawa on the qānūn and Suzanne Meyers Sawa on the darabukka and tambourine.

The events of the conference and the publication of the proceedings were made possible by the generosity of The Social Sciences and Humanities Research Council of Canada, and the following institutions and officers of The University of Toronto: the Principal of University College, the President of Victoria University, the Centre for Reformation and Renaissance Studies at Victoria College, the Centre for Medieval Studies, the Dean of the Faculty of Music, the Vice-President and Provost of the University. On behalf of everyone, I express our sincere gratitude.

Organizing the conference would not have been possible without the support of the members of the Conference on Editorial Problems, whose expertise and good will made the rough places plain. Special thanks to G. E. Bentley Jr., an intrepid chair, to John N. Grant, an able treasurer, and to Janet Paterson, an adroit manager of local arrangements.

The typesetting for this volume was done by Mike Dunleavy of Humanities Publishing Services of the University of Toronto. A grant from the Humanities and Social Sciences Committee of the University of Toronto made it possible for Brian E. Power to proof-read and copy-edit the text.

M.R.M.
1991

Music Discourse from Classical to Early Modern Times

Fidelities and Infidelities in Translating Early Music Theory

Claude V. Palisca,
Yale University

To what in the original text should a translation be faithful—to the author's terminology by the use of cognates?—to the syntax? —to sentence-structure and paragraphing?—to the images?—to the general sense?—to every nuance of the author's message?— to the author's writing style?

TERMINOLOGY. The technical language of music theory is full of terms that have different meanings today from what they had in earlier times. The most problematic of these terms is "harmony." In the earliest writings—both Greek and Latin—*harmonia* stood for agreement of parts and relations as well as for the more particularly musical agreement of pitches related through consonance or through belonging to a certain mode or scale. This agreement was manifested in appealing melody. The act of creating melody, whether by a performer extempore or by a composer in writing, was represented by a form of the verb *modulare*. Many of the older and some of the recent translations render these terms in English as "harmony" and "modulate." This is harmless enough, if it is made clear that these English terms stand for the earlier meanings. But since passages from translations are frequently quoted out of context without the annotations supporting them, and theoretical works are rarely read from beginning to end, the passages in which these English equivalents occur are subject to misinterpretation.

If in a particular context the translator determines that a medieval author meant by *harmonia* melody and by *modulare* to make melody, it seems decidedly preferable to say in the translation "melody" and "to make melody" rather than to preserve "harmony" and "modulate." To be sure, the cognate is lost—whatever that is worth—but we are free of the ambiguity too.

If we move up to the sixteenth century, the situation becomes even more confusing. Gioseffo Zarlino uses *harmonia* both in the older sense of general agreement of members and for the coordinated movement of independent voices that accord with one another through consonances. He also uses the term *melodia*, but not for "melody" (which is usually *modulatione*). The Italian *melodia* captures the sense of Plato's *melos*—a mixture of text, rhythm and compatible pitches, the latter concept extended by Zarlino to both successive and simultaneous combinations. It would be wrong to translate *melodia* as "melody;" *melos* would not mean much to a modern reader. "Song" usually fits best, though not in every situation.

You may think that what I just stated about terminology is pretty obvious. But actually it is controversial. Thomas J. Mathiesen and Jon Solomon, who like I, edit a series of translations, though one limited to Greek and Latin treatises, in 1982 promulgated guidelines for their series that contain the statement:

> Technical terminology will be rendered "by the corresponding English term in an equivalent, congruent technical terminology,"[1] even though it may be somewhat obsolete in terms of modern usage. The English terminology adopted must be used consistently for the corresponding Greek or Latin terms throughout the translation.[2]

Following this principle, if an author at different times and in different contexts used the term *harmonia* for harmony of the universe, for melodic pitch relationships, and for simultaneous consonance, we should translate *harmonia* always by the same word or expression, probably "harmony," even though the translation would be more transparent if the English terms were respectively "cosmic harmony," "melody," and "consonance." I believe that the goal of transparency and immediate comprehension takes precedence over consistency of verbal equivalence.

Another problem with verbal equivalence is that the best authors were deliberately inconsistent. Like modern authors, they considered it gauche to use the same term all the time, when synonyms could make the prose more varied. For example, Boethius in one chapter in *De institutione musice* (2.7) used three different words for "ratio," *proportio*, *habitudo*, and *comparatio*, although it is obvious that he meant the same thing by all three. A translator could equate *proportio* with "proportion," *habitudo* with "ratio," and *comparatio* with "relation," or some other set of equivalents. But there is neither compulsion to do this nor any particular advantage gained, because the only good English word for any of the Latin terms is "ratio."

Another pitfall of consistency results from the poverty of technical vocabulary available to earlier writers. Latin terms such as *vox*, *corda*, *sonus*, and *figura*, and the Italian *voce* and *nota*, stood for a range of concepts that in today's terminology have specific designations. Thus *vox* could be translated as "pitch," but when the author says that a *vox* rises or descends, this cannot be "a pitch," because we understand a pitch as a discrete frequency; if it is altered, that is, rises or falls, it becomes a different pitch. A pitch can neither rise nor fall. A better alternate for *vox* then would be "step," because you can go up or down a step. In different contexts, therefore, *vox* might be best represented by "pitch," "note," "step," "voice," "solmization syllable," or something else. *Figura* may stand for "note-head," "note-shape," "note-value," a "sign," such as flat, sharp, or clef, but not "figure," unless it refers to a diagram or graphic representation.

One of the expressions I find most offensive is "figured music" or "figural music" for *musica figurata*. "Figured music" evokes an image of music saturated with runs and arpeggios, whereas *musica figurata* was music written with *figurae*, instead of *punctae* or *neumae*, that is, music written with note-shapes having determinate note-values, in other words, "measured music." Most often the connotation of *musica figurata* is simply "polyphonic music."

A translation will not hit its mark unless it is expressed in the language that the translator and readers share, and that includes the technical terminology in vogue in our own time. Johann Christoph Gottsched expressed this well when he said:

> Zunächst freilich scheint die oft wiederholte Maxime: der übersetzte Autor müsse zu uns reden, wie er als Deutscher zu Deutschen reden würde.[3]

SYNTAX. Let us now consider the formal aspects of the text to be translated—paragraphing, sentence-structure, tenses, indicative, subjunctive, and conditional moods, active and passive voices, connective particles, indefinite and definite articles, indefinite pronouns (such as "someone" or "one").

Older texts are notoriously deficient in paragraphing. This is most lacking in texts whose original sources are manuscripts, but paragraphing continues to be scarce in early printed sources. The most glaring example I can think of is Vincenzo Galilei's *Discorso intorno all'opere di messer Gioseffo Zarlino da Chioggia* (Florence: Giorgio Marescotti, 1589). From page 7, where the discourse begins, to page 134, where it ends, there is only a single paragraph break, on page 90, because there Galilei introduces a table. In place of paragraphing, Galilei uses certain phrases, such as *Hora* ("Now"), *Vengo hora* ("I come now"), and *Tornando* ("Turning"). However, even these signposts are not frequent enough to provide the breaks expected by a modern reader. The translator has to divide the unbroken effusion of words into rational units consistent with modern practice.

Latin and old Italian texts depend a great deal on connective particles to make the prose flow. We are used to having one thought follow another without continuously inserting "and," "but," "furthermore," "consequently," "therefore," and so on. Many of these particles found in the text may be omitted in the translation. Often, indeed, the "but" does not introduce anything in opposition to the previous statement, and the "therefore" precedes something that is not a logical consequent of the previous statement. The translator must question every such particle and eliminate most of them, particularly the initial "And."

Latin authors and those influenced by the ancient languages wrote notoriously long sentences. Languages with declensions and gender permit more complex organization of sentences, because the agreement of word endings promotes clarity and economy of reference. In English, since nouns and pronouns need to be repeated to make clear the identity of the subjects and objects, the writer tends to break up thoughts into smaller units. The long sentences of the original text should be broken up into the kind of statements normal to modern English writing. Some may object that the prose will lose its quaint, archaic character. But why should it be archaic, since it is the product of a modern translator-writer? Not all the complexity of sentence-structure in early music treatises is owed to the characteristics of the language and of the time. Much of it comes from the original author's failure to write crisply and the absence of an experienced editor. In this connection I should remark that the translations published in Oliver Strunk's *Source Readings in Music History*, as valuable as this venerable anthology is, tend to preserve the older sentence-structure, and should not always be considered models.

In English, we use the subjunctive and conditional moods and the presumptive future tense less frequently than even modern European writers. The older texts are laden with these, and any translator who observes them indiscriminately will sound stilted and lame.

The discourse on how to perform tragedy I have attributed to Giovanni Bardi begins with a flood of subjunctives, and in a literal translations goes:

> It is reasonable that, wishing to make a discourse on how one ought to perform tragedy, that we should recall the ancient, so that we might be able, if not to make it appear as supremely magnificent theater . . . that at least it should not be unworthy of its beauties and features.

In my published translation this is simplified to:

> It is reasonable that, wishing to discuss how to perform tragedy, we should recall the ancient [tragedy]. Thus we may perhaps not make ours appear as supremely magnificent theater . . . yet at least perform it in a way not unworthy of its beauties and features.[4]

Here is a sentence by Nicola Vicentino in which the future tense is used to suppose a compositional scenario:

> Oltre di ciò il Compositore auuertirà, quando egli uorrà notare le pause, scriuerà quelle in tal ordine, che faccino bel uedere al Cantante; . . .[5]

Translated literally it becomes:

> Besides this, the composer will take note, that when he will notate the rests, he will write them in such an order that they might be made good to see by the singer.

This entire statement should be changed to the present indicative:

> A composer should take care, when writing rests, to set them out in an order that will look attractive to the singer.

Most European languages use the construction "one does," "one knows," etc. Such expressions as *on dit que* or *on fait* fall naturally on the tongue, as do *si dice* or *si deve fare così*. But in English the parallel usage is unidiomatic. It is more natural to say "we" or "you." The translator should take the liberty of changing "one" to "we" or "you" or to turn the sentence around to the passive voice: "It is said" or "This is done."

MEANING. How closely need the translator adhere to the meaning of the original? May he or she introduce interpretation by adding explanatory phrases or missing steps in the logic? No, the translator may not introduce anything that is not in the original. Nor may he or she omit anything that is in the original. The translation must reflect every nuance and detail of the original. But this can be done without hanging on every word of the text. Translating words rather than thoughts leads to "translatorese," the name John Ciardi gave to that queer "language-of-the-study" that counts words but misses their living force.[6]

Occasionally the translator will have to add a word or phrase to make clear a thought that is incompletely expressed in the original. This may be added in brackets. However, as long as the translator is communicating the original content, he or she may add as many words as are necessary, even when their equivalents are not in the original.

STYLE. In a literary work, the translator wants to convey not only the message of the author, but also the author's way of thinking and speaking, the artistic personality. This is also important in works of music theory. If the translator is faithful to the author's every turn of thought, even if not every turn of phrase, this personality will come through. When the author is made to appear as a native speaker of American English, it is still his or her style—not the translator's—that is realized in the ultimate product.

I shall now apply some of these criteria to three excerpts from published translations.

Example 1
Anonymous, *His ita perspectis*[7]

A = Anonymous   MAL = Mark A. Leach   CVP = the author

A   *Notandum enim   quia nulla vox habet ultra*
MAL For it should be noted that no pitch has more than
CVP It should be observed that from no step can you

A   *quattuor eleuationes uel depositiones. quia nulla vox potest*
MAL four elevations   or depositions,   because no pitch can
CVP rise or fall more than four steps,   because from any step

A   *eleuari uel deponi.   nisi   ad secunda et tertiam. quartam*
MAL be raised or lowered unless to the second or third, or fourth
CVP you cannot go up or down except to a second, third, fourth,

A   *vel quintam.   Omnes quoque voces*
MAL or fifth [pitch above or below]. In addition, all pitches
CVP or fifth step.   Moreover, you

A   *has quattuor eleuationes vel depositiones habere non possunt.*
MAL cannot have these four elevations or depositions;
CVP cannot go up or down these four steps from every step.

A   *quam quare ita sit alia si requiras inuenies.*
MAL why it may be so you will find elsewhere if you should require.
CVP The reason for this, if you need it, you will find elsewhere.

A   *Habebis itaque quattuor eleuationes uel depositiones in voce*
MAL And so you will have four elevations or depositions on the
CVP Thus you can go up or down four steps from the

A   *prima.   tertia. uel quarta.   [septima.]   In*
MAL first,   third,   fourth,   or seventh pitch.   On the
CVP first [A], third [C], fourth [D], or seventh step [G]. From

A   *secunda eleuationes tres depositiones duas.*
MAL second [pitch there are] three elevations, two depositions.
CVP the second [B] you can go up three and down two.

A   *In quinta eleuationes tres. et depositiones quattuor.*
MAL On the fifth [pitch there are] three elevations and four
CVP From the fifth step [E] you can go up three and down four.

A   *In sexta eleuationes duas.*
MAL   depositions. On the sixth [pitch there are] two elevations,
CVP   From the sixth step [F] you have two steps up

A   *depositiones tres. Ecce ad hunc exemplum eleuatur omnis*
MAL   three depositions. Behold: every
CVP   and three down.   In this example, then,   every

A   *neuma uocis*   *primae*   *uel*
MAL   *neuma* (i.e., every pitch group) of the first   or
CVP   neum that starts   on the first step [A], or the

A   *quartae.*   *A.D.*
MAL   fourth pitch is elevated in this example. A.D.
CVP   fourth step [D], rises.

The published translation is a good example of merely sub-stituting English words for Latin words, confounding the English reader of music theory with newly invented technical language, foreign words, needless subjunctives, misused currently accepted terms, and unnecessary parenthetical verbiage and remarks. Most important, it fails to get the meaning across on a first or second, or even a third reading. It has the character of a pony or crib, the surreptitious crutches used by students of Latin. It is a grammatically correct recitation of the words that, delivered orally, would probably satisfy a secondary-school Latin teacher. But it puts unnecessary obstacles in the way of a non-reader of Latin. No modern speakers of English would ever express themselves this way. I have tried to render in everyday English what the anonymous writer wanted to get across, neither adding nor subtracting anything significant, but without regard for word-for-word correspondence. Although it may be of some interest to readers of Latin theory that this author uses *elevationes* and *depositiones* for upward and downward steps, this is not necessarily relevant to someone who seeks to know what this commentator on Guido's letter to Brother Michael is saying in order to clarify or elaborate upon that text, which is partially translated in Strunk's book.[8] Guido's letter should receive, one of these days, a complete and, I hope, transparent translation.

A passage that has received a variety of translations is Johannes Tinctoris' definition of what distinguished written composition from unwritten counterpoint. Below I give the excerpt in Albert Seay's Latin edition[9] and in his translation,[10] then in my translation.

Example 2
Johannes Tinctoris, *Liber de arte contrapuncti*[11]
JT = Johannes Tinctoris   AS = Albert Seay   CVP = the author

JT   2 *Porro tam simplex quam diminutus contrapuctus*
AS   Continuing, both simple, as well as diminuted counterpoint,
CVP   Both simple and diminished counterpoint

JT   *dupliciter fit,*   *hoc est aut scripto aut*
AS   is made in a double manner, that is either written out or
CVP   are made in two ways,   namely, either written or

JT   *mente.*   3 *Contrapunctus qui scripto fit communiter*
AS   improvised.   Counterpoint which is written out is commonly
CVP   mentally.   A counterpoint made in writing is commonly

JT   *res facta nominatur.*   4 *At istum quem mentaliter*
AS   named composed (*res facta*).   But that which we do mentally.
CVP   called "a composed work."   But that which we fashion

JT   *conficimus absolute contrapunctum vocamus, et hunc qui*
AS   we call absolute counterpoint   and those who
CVP   mentally we call simply "counterpoint,"   and those who

JT   *faciunt super librum cantare vulgariter dicuntur.*
AS   do this are said vulgarly to sing *super librum.*
CVP   make it are colloquially said "to sing from a chantbook."

JT   5 *In hoc autem res facta a contrapuncto potissimum differt,*
AS   In this, however, composition differs from counterpoint,
CVP   A composed work differs from a counterpoint mainly

JT   *quod omnes partes rei factae*   *sive tres sive*
AS   since all the parts of composed music, be they three, or
CVP   in that all the parts of a composed work, whether three,

JT   *quatuor sive plures sint, sibi mutuo obligentur,*   *ita*
AS   four, or many, are mutually interdependent,   so
CVP   four, or more, are mutually responsible to each other, in

JT   *quod ordo lexque concordantiarum cuiuslibet partis erga*
AS   that the order and law of concords of any part in relation
CVP   that the succession and rule of concords of any part must be

JT   *singulas et omnes observari debeat,*   *ut*
AS   to themselves and all the others should be observed as is
CVP   observed towards each and all parts,   as is

JT   *satis patet in hoc exemplo quinque partium existenti,*
AS   seen satisfactorily in this example written in five parts;
CVP   sufficiently clear in this example completed in five parts;

JT   *quarumquidem partium tres primo,*   *deinde quatuor ac*
AS   of these parts, three sing at the beginning, then four,   and
CVP   of these parts, three sing at the beginning, then four,   and

JT   *postremo omnes quinque concinunt:*
AS   then finally, all five:
CVP   finally all five:

A number of the published translations of this chapter, notably that of Margaret Bent,[12] preserve the Latin terms *res facta* and *cantare super librum*. Although I might give these Latin terms in a footnote or even in brackets beside the English terms, I believe a translation should be entirely in English. Tinctoris himself happens to give a definition of *res facta* in his *Terminorum musicae diffinitorium* (Naples *ca.* 1472/73). He says it is equivalent to *cantus compositus*. He also defines *cantus* and *cantus compositus*. *Cantus compositus*, he writes, "which is commonly called *resfacta*, is that which is set forth (*editus*) through the manifold relationships of the notes of one part to those of another."[13] Essentially, then, a *cantus compositus* or a *res facta* is a written work of polyphonic music. Since the chapter is about polyphony, it is sufficient to translate *res facta* as "a composed work," the adjective "composed" distinguishing it from counterpoint produced *mentaliter* or mentally. Here, "mentally" means not written down. Seay interpreted *mente* in sentence 2 to mean "improvised," whereas in sentence 4 he translated *mentaliter* as "mentally." How impromptu or improvised this "mental" music was depended on how often the same singers made counterpoint together on a given chant. With repeated rehearsals, they may well have worked out a set of counterpoints that they kept in their heads, hence still *mentaliter*, but no longer impromptu. I have therefore, avoided reading "improvised" into the definition.

In sentence 3, I translated *contrapunctus* as "a counterpoint," because Tinctoris defines *contrapunctus* as *cantus*, which suggests that he meant "a vocal piece" and not a process. Besides, a process cannot be a *res*, a thing.

In sentence 5, I expanded *librum* to "chantbook," because it was no ordinary book. It was, in fact, a "choirbook," a large book of chants from which a small choir could read. I chose "chantbook" rather than "choirbook" on the grounds that it might not be clear to everyone that a choirbook did not contain polyphony.

I have omitted translating connective words such as *Porro* in sentence 2, and *In hoc autem* in sentence 5. They are superfluous.

Of course, this is not the only viable translation of this passage. But it does satisfy my criteria of faithful transference of the thought content in its every essential detail and nuance into plain and normal English, without coining new expressions or assimilating foreign terms.

Let us consider an example in Italian that involves some of the terms I discussed earlier. It is from Zarlino's *Le Istitutioni harmoniche*, Book 3, chapter 1. Below I present an actual early draft that was revised to produce the translation published in 1968 by the Yale University Press as *The Art of Counterpoint*.[14] Underlined English words in the draft were eliminated or replaced in the published version by the words on the line above.

Example 3
Gioseffo Zarlino, *Le Istitutioni harmoniche*[15]

PV = published version   ED = early draft   GZ = Gioseffo Zarlino

PV
ED   I consider   counterpoint to be that   concordance   or
GZ 1 *Dico adunque che Contrapunto è*   *quella Concordanza, o*

PV   agreement
ED   harmony   which is born of a body with
GZ 2 *concento, che da vn corpo,*   *ilquale habbia in se*

PV   melodic lines
ED   diverse parts, its various modulations   accommodated
GZ 3 *diuerse parti, & diuerse modulationi   accommodate*

PV   total composition,   so that   are
ED   to the melody,   arranged with   the voices
GZ 4 *alla cantilena,   ordinate con   uoci*

PV   commensurable,
ED   separated by commensurate, harmonious, intervals. . . . .
GZ 5 *distanti l'vna dall'altra per interualli comensurabili, &*

PV   also
ED   It might even be said that counterpoint is
GZ 6 *harmonici. . . . . Si può anche dire, che'l Contrapunto sia*

PV   that
ED   a kind of harmony   which contains diverse variations of
GZ 7 *vn modo di harmonia, che contenghi in se diuerse variationi de*

PV   steps,   using   rational intervallic
ED   sounds or voices,   with certain reasonable
GZ 8 *suoni, o de voci   cantabili, con certa   ragione di*

PV   temporal measurements. . . . Diminished
ED   proportions and measure. . . .   But diminished
GZ 9 *proportioni, &   misura di tempo. . . .   Ma il Diminuito,*

PV
ED   counterpoint has dissonances   as well as
GZ 10 *non solo hà le parti composte di Consonanze, ma etiandio*

PV   employ every kind of note-value
ED   consonances   and may <u>have any kind of figure</u>
GZ 11 *di Dissonanze; & in esso si pone ogni sorte di figure*

PV   as the composer wishes.   It
ED   <u>desired by the composer;</u>   <u>Its</u>
GZ 12 *cantabile, secondo l'arbitrio del Compositore; & le sue*

PV   proceeds   by intervals or
ED   <u>modulations are organized</u> <u>in intervals and</u>
GZ 13   *modulationi sono ordinate per interualli, o*

PV   singable spaces,   values   reckoned
ED   <u>rests,</u>   and its <u>figures</u> are <u>numbered</u> according
GZ 14 *spacij cantabili; & le figure   numerate secondo*

PV   measure of its tempus.
ED   to the <u>tempus of the measure.</u>
GZ 15   *la misura del Tempo.*

In the draft a number of key words were mistranslated, sometimes by cognates that no longer evoke the image that Zarlino's words were intended to communicate. At other times the translator was snared by traps in Zarlino's archaic language. In line 2, *concento* could mean "harmony," but here "agreement" comes closer. In line 3, "modulations" are, of course, melodic lines, and *cantilena* in line 4 cannot mean "melody" in the modern sense, since the subject is polyphonic music. "Harmony" fits line 7, because Zarlino earlier defines harmony in a way consistent with this and our usage. In line 8, *voci cantabili* does not refer to voices but rather to pitches or steps of the scale. "Reasonable" proportions is wrong in line 8, because Zarlino is alluding to ratios made up of whole numbers and therefore rational. *Misura di tempo* in line 9 denotes a general mensuration of time. In line 11, *figure* is, of course, not "figures" but "note-values." *Spacij cantabili* in line 14 are spatial distances that the singer traverses, or "singable spaces." *La misura del tempo* in line 15 seems to refer to the measurement of the tempus, which was the relation between the breve and semibreve, the most fundamental relationship in the conventional *alla breve* measure, consisting of downbeat and upbeat, each worth a semi-breve.

This passage is full of pitfalls, and I am not sure that our published solution avoided all of them. However, it illustrates very cogently how important it is to analyze the old terminology in terms of its context and usage, and then to find in our musical parlance appropriate means to express it.

The most important stage in the translating process may be that moment when the translator puts the original away and contemplates the work as a piece of writing in his or her own language. The translator's draft should say clearly in the ordinary language of the music theorist's profession what the original author intended. If a passage is unclear or unidiomatic, this is the time to improve it. The original author may have been obscure or awkward. The translator may not be. Even if the original is impenetrable, the translator must take a position by interpreting the passage. The interpretation need not be defended in a note. The translator of a treatise must be equipped not only to translate the words but also to interpret them, and must accept this responsibility. The reader looks to the translator as the authority on the author's text and will be disappointed if this responsibility is passed on to the reader unschooled in the author's linguistic conventions. The fidelity that matters is in the message, and this depends on understanding it and being able to transmit it with authentic vigor concisely and transparently.

NOTES

1. Quoted from a review by R. Mathiesen in *Language* 51/3 (1975) 733.

2. T. J. Mathiesen and J. Solomon *Greek and Latin Music Theory, A Style Guide for Text Criticism, Translation, and the Preparation of Camera-ready Typescript* (Lincoln and London 1982) 13.

3. Quoted in W. Schadewaldt "Das Problem des Übersetzens" in *Das Problem des Übersetzens* ed. H. J. Störig (Stuttgart 1963) 253, (Darmstadt 1973) 227. "Above all the often repeated maxim certainly

stands out: the translated author should speak to us as if a German were speaking to Germans."

4. Giovanni Bardi (?) "[Discourse on how Tragedy should be Performed]" in *The Florentine Camerata: Documentary Studies and Translations* by C. V. Palisca (New Haven and London 1989) 140–1.

5. Nicola Vicentino *L'antica musica ridotta alla moderna prattica* (Rome 1555) IV, 7 f.75v.

6. Quoted in B. Q. Morgan "Bibliography," in *On Translation* ed. R. A. Brower (Cambridge, Mass. 1959) 290.

7. Florence: Biblioteca Nazionale Centrale, MS Conventi soppressi F III 565 (*ca.* 1100) ed. M. A. Leach in " 'His ita perspectis': A Practical Supplement to Guido of Arezzo's Pedagogical Method" *Journal of Musicology* 8 (1990) 87–90.

8. O. Strunk *Source Readings in Music History: From Classical Antiquity through the Romantic Era* (New York 1950) 125.

9. *Johannis Tinctoris opera theoretica* **Corpus scriptorum de musica** 22 (American Institute of Musicology 1975) 2:107.

10. *The Art of Counterpoint* trans. and ed. with an Introduction by A. Seay (American Institute of Musicology 1961) 102–3.

11. (Naples 1477) II, 20.

12. "*Resfacta* and *Cantare Super Librum*" *Journal of the American Musicological Society* 36 (1983) 371–3.

13. *Terminorum musicae diffinitorium* ed. and trans. by A. Machabey (Paris 1951) 10.

14. *The Art of Counterpoint, Part Three of Le Istitutioni harmoniche, 1558* trans. G. A. Marco and C. V. Palisca (New Haven and London 1968; New York 1976 and 1983) 1–2.

15. (Venice 1558) 147.

Editing Adémar de Chabannes' Liturgy for the Feast of Saint Martial

James Grier
Yale University

On 3 August 1029, the monks of the Abbey of Saint Martial in Limoges sought to inaugurate a new liturgy for their patron saint, a new liturgy that acknowledged and celebrated his status as an apostle, the younger cousin of Simon Peter, an intimate of Jesus himself, and Saint Peter's delegate to Gaul.[1] The historical Martial was well-known, from the writings of Gregory of Tours, as a third-century Roman missionary to Limoges who became its first Bishop, and the liturgy that the apostolic version replaced clearly recognized him as a confessor-bishop.[2] The motivation to create this far-fetched tale of his apostolicity was twofold: the desire to increase the appeal of Limoges, and particularly the Abbey dedicated to the newly-coined apostle, as a pilgrimage destination; and to augment the prestige of the city's rival ecclesiastical institution, the Cathedral of Saint Stephen, as the only apostolic seat in Gaul.[3] As such it found widespread acceptance and support among the people of Limoges, most notably the bishop Jordan, despite the ardent and sometimes strident opposition of the Cathedral's canons to Martial's apostolic status and the attendant distinction that would accrue to the sepulchre of the new apostle, the Abbey of Saint Martial.[4] It is a measure of the degree of the bishop's accord that the ceremony took place not only in the Cathedral itself but also on the feast of both the Invention of Saint Stephen (celebrated on 3 August throughout the western church) and the Dedication of the Cathedral.[5] Unfortunately, the première met a disastrous result. A monk from Lombardy, Benedict of Chiusa, apparently with some encouragement from the canons of Saint Stephen's, appeared just as the Mass was beginning and began an outcry, condemning the apostolicity of Martial and his new liturgy as offensive to God. He spoke in the vernacular, and his arguments swayed the assembled crowd. The outcome of this fiasco was the suppression of the new apostolic liturgy for two decades or more.

A key figure on the Abbey's side of the story and interlocutor with Benedict on the fateful day of 3 August 1029 is Adémar de Chabannes, monk at Saint Cybard in Angoulême and at Saint Martial of Limoges in the first third of the eleventh century, and well known as an historian, homilist and polemicist.[6] Moreover, the principle source for the apostolic liturgy, portions of Paris, Bibliothèque Nationale, latin 909 (hereafter Pa 909), are written in Adémar's own hand, both text and music.[7] Adémar is also the author of the account of the events of 3 August 1029, narrated in a circular letter addressed, but probably never sent, to prominent clerics in Limoges and throughout Aquitaine, Duke William of Aquitaine, the Dowager Empress Kunigunde, the German Emperor Conrad II, and Pope John XIX. The epistle, which survives in autograph, details Adémar's debate with Benedict, his subsequent disgrace and departure from Saint Martial to his former Abbey of Saint Cybard the day after, and the ongoing polemic about Martial's apostolicity in which Adémar engaged from his new, and old, home in Angoulême.[8] This tempestuous monk, then, was intimately involved with the creation of the apostolic liturgy for Saint Martial, and with the preparation for its inauguration in August 1029. Here I intend to examine the procedures Adémar employed in composing this new liturgy, his motivation for adopting these methods, and the implications of these factors for those who would edit this material.

Codex Pa 909 is a typical Aquitanian musico-liturgical manuscript of the early eleventh century. It contains several component sections, each of which transmits a distinct liturgical category of piece. These sections are usually termed *libelli* ("little books") in modern codicological parlance, and their contents are summarized in Table 1. The order of several gatherings following f.109 was disrupted during an earlier rebinding and the most recent restoration in 1979 resulted in the misplacement of a further gathering. The earlier misbinding is well documented in the literature on this codex, and for convenience I include details here.[9] The more recent disruption is of some importance to my argument, and I shall discuss it below. In its original form, this codex was written certainly in Limoges and, I believe, in the scriptorium of Saint Martial for use in the neighboring house dedicated to Saint Martin.[10] Its creation, however, was interrupted at quite an advanced stage. The signatures, entered on the bottom center verso of the last folio of eleven gatherings in the codex, provide evidence first of the careful planning under which the manuscript was executed and second the disruption of that plan. First, the libelli that were intended to make up the latter part of the codex bear no signatures in their constituent gatherings: antiphons of Easter, Tracts, Offertories, Processional Antiphons, the tonary and antiphonal. Second, two pieces of evidence show that the libellus of Proper tropes was left incomplete by the original scribe. Musical notation and rubrication, missing from two trope complexes already on f.57v, are not entered from f.58r and the hand of the original scribe breaks off altogether partway down f.59r, on the third folio of what would be gathering G, at the end of tropes for Saint Androchius. This gathering, then, was left incomplete and unsigned by the original scribe. The second

Table 1
Summary Inventory and Gathering Structure of Pa 909

Folios	Signature	Inventory
1–8	none	Miscellaneous additions
9–16	A	Proper tropes
17–24	B	Proper tropes
25–32	C	Proper tropes
33–40	D	Proper tropes
49–56	F	Proper tropes
41–48	**none**	**Proper tropes**
		ff.42–46 Troped Mass for Saint Martial
57–64	none	ff.57–59r Proper tropes
		ff.59–61 Proper tropes
		ff.61v–62r Alleluias for Saint Martial
		ff.62v Vespers for Saint Martial
65–72	**none**	**ff.62v–68 Matins for Saint Martial**
		ff.68v–69 Lauds for Saint Martial
		ff.69v–70r Antiphons for Saint Martial
		f.70r Second Vespers for Saint Martial
		ff.70v–71 Untroped Mass for Saint Martial
		ff.71v–72r Tract for Saint Martial
73–81	**none**	**ff.72–74 Antiphons and Responsories for Saint Martial**
		ff.75–77 Prosae (*two for Saint Martial*)
		f.78 Palimpsest: miscellaneous additions
82–85	**none**	**ff.79–85 Offices for Saints Valery and Austriclinian**
86–93	I	Ordinary tropes
94–101	K	Ordinary tropes
102–109	L	Ordinary tropes
110–117	**none**	**Sequentiae**
118–125	**none**	**Sequentiae**
		ff.118–119 Sequentiae for Saint Martial
126–133	none	Tracts
134–141	none	Tracts, Benedictions, Litany, Antiphons

142–149	none	Miscellaneous items for Easter
150–157	none	Processional antiphons
158–165	none	Processional antiphons
166–173	none	Alleluias, Trope for Saint Clement, Antiphons for Easter
174–181	N	Alleluias
		ff.177v–178r Alleluias for Saint Martial
182–189	O	Alleluias
190–197	M	Alleluias
198–205	**none**	**Sequentiae**
		ff.198–201 Prosae for Saint Martial
		ff.202–205r **Versus de Sancto Marciale**
		LXXta IIo
206–213	none	Offertories
214–221	none	Offertories
222–229	none	Offertories
230–237	none	Offertories
238–245	none	Offertories
246–253	none	Processional antiphons
		f.251r Processional antiphon for Saint Martial
254–261	none	ff.251–257 Tonary: **additions by Adémar**
262–269	none	ff.258–269 Antiphons

indication that the making of this libellus was interrupted is the absence of initials, where space had been provided for them, at the beginning of several feasts; in other places initials do not fill all the space left for them.[11]

The cause for this discontinuation was Adémar's need for a codex in which to place his newly created apostolic liturgy for Saint Martial. He obtained the book, probably as it was nearing completion in the scriptorium of the Abbey of Saint Martial as a commission from the neighboring Abbey of Saint Martin, and made entries in six places in the book. These additions are marked in bold in Table 1. First, he substituted for the original and now lost gathering E of the libellus of Proper tropes a new unsigned gathering whose principal concern is the tropes for the Mass of Saint Martial. Other tropes precede and follow this Mass in such a way that the continuity between the original gatherings D and F is not interrupted. Unfortunately, as a result of the restoration of 1979, this substitute gathering is now misplaced between gathering F and that which would have been signed G. I dwell on this accident because it obscures a key piece of evidence for the relationship between Pa 909 and 1119, a troper also from Saint Martial, but dating from the middle of the eleventh century. Gathering F opens in the middle of *Quia naturam*, a trope for the Assumption, and the first word of the gathering is *mortis*. When Adémar copied his substitute for original gathering E, he had just a little too much space at the end and so he wrote the word *mortis*, the first word of the next gathering, to fill in the space. This dittography appears also in Pa 1119's version of *Quia naturam*, a sure proof that it is a direct copy of Pa 909, at least for this portion of its repertory. Because of the current misplacement of Adémar's gathering in Pa 909, the repetition of *mortis* is no longer visible at a glance.[12]

Adémar's second contribution is the continuation of the libellus of Proper tropes from the end of the unfinished gathering G. Here he entered tropes for several Masses, including the Translation of Saint Benedict, which ought to follow the feast of Saint

Martial; sufficient space was not available in Adémar's substitute gathering, and so he deferred these tropes to the end of the libellus.[13] There follows a collection of six Alleluias with verse for Saint Martial and then Adémar's *chef d'œuvre* for the feast of his house's patron, a complete apostolic liturgy including the principal Offices, an untroped Mass Proper, a Tract, processional antiphons, and two prosae. This section of the codex closes with newly composed Offices for Saints Valery and Austriclinian, companions of Martial. As well as filling the folios of gathering G left blank by the interruption of its original scribe's work, Adémar created three new gatherings to hold this material. In the process, the original gathering H, which was the first in the libellus of Ordinary tropes, was lost.[14]

Third, Adémar added a complete sequentiary for the entire liturgical year, at the end of which he wrote two further prosae for Saint Martial and the famous seventy-two verses for the Apostle, well-known from Paul Hooreman's study published forty years ago.[15] His fourth and fifth additions consist of two further Alleluias for Saint Martial added over an erasure in the libellus of Alleluias, and an antiphon entered the same way into the libellus of processional antiphons. His sixth and final set of entries occurs in the tonary, where several incipits are erased and some additions in Adémar's hand are to be found.[16] To this corpus of material in Pa 909 can be added one further source, a bifolium in Adémar's hand, placed at the end of Pa 1978. This is an inner bifolium, either the second or third, of a quaternio, the rest of which is now lost, and which originally contained an Office for Saint Cybard, the patron of Adémar's other monastery in Angoulême, and one or more Offices for Saint Martial. The fragment of the latter accords very closely with the version preserved in Pa 909.[17]

What is remarkable about these documents is that Adémar collected, into a single series, all or most of the music necessary for the performance of the liturgy on individual feasts: three in Pa 909 (Saints Martial, Valery, and Austriclinian), and two in Pa 1978 (Saints Martial and Cybard, whose feasts, incidentally, fall on 30 June and 1 July, respectively). This arrangement is not without precedent in Aquitaine: similar libelli devoted to a single feast have been discovered in Pa 1240, which carries the Office for Sainte Foy de Conques (ff.185–188), and Pa 2826, which transmits tropes and proses for the feast of Saint Géraud d'Aurillac (ff.2–3).[18] Nevertheless, it is certainly not the usual arrangement for the transmission of liturgical music in Aquitaine at this period; more common is the division of the pieces into liturgical categories and the assignment of these categories to independent libelli, as mentioned above. For the editor, however, Adémar's arrangement greatly simplifies matters: we have an autograph that is complete and consistent in the matters of text, music, and rubrics. One would expect to make a diplomatic transcription, regularize capitalization and punctuation, and send it to the printer. Nevertheless, more than one *crux*, to use the parlance of textual criticism, confronts the editor who would wish to give his or her audience some guidance in understanding these texts and the use to which they were put.

I shall restrict my comments here to the Mass texts; their problems are sufficiently vexing to occupy the balance of this paper. The Office texts are equally interesting and troublesome, and they certainly deserve an independent study. Let us now consider the corpus of items for the Mass with which Adémar provides us. These are indicated in italics in Table 1. Two observations need to be made: Adémar compiled two complete Propers for the Mass (one troped, the other untroped, but each also varying in the responsorial chants, Gradual and Alleluia), and a large number of Alleluias; to these latter can be added one Tract.[19] Plates I and II show the opening of the troped and untroped Masses, respectively, for the feast of Saint Martial. What was Adémar's motivation for collecting such a large group of texts? In the early eleventh century, three feasts were observed during the liturgical year for the Abbey's patron (see Table 2),

Table 2
Feasts for Saint Martial Celebrated at the Abbey of Saint Martial in
Limoges *ca*. A.D. 1000, taken from the Kalendar of Pa 1240

30 June	*Marcialis*
7 July	*Octabas sancti marcialis*
10 October	*Translacio sancti marcialis*

and it would seem that Adémar is merely providing alternatives,
especially in the matter of Alleluias, for these occasions.

As Table 2 shows, however, none of these three feasts falls
within Lent, and so the function of the Tract *Marcialem apostolum Petrus*, whose introductory rubric assigns it to Lent, is
unclear. Certainly the most important of these feasts is the com-
memoration of the Saint's death, 30 June, and the extravagantly
troped version of the Mass belongs to this day: it appears in the
libellus of Proper tropes between the feast of the Commemora-
tion of Saint Paul (30 June) and the feast of Saint Lawrence (10
August); in all likelihood, the tropes for the Translation of Saint
Benedict (11 July) should precede Saint Lawrence directly, as
mentioned above, and so further narrow the range of dates available for Martial's feast. The untroped Mass, then, might have
been used for the Translation or Octave. I shall return to the
tropes themselves momentarily.

First, however, we must also consider the other differences
in the two Masses, specifically the Gradual and Alleluia. Their
sources and origin suggest another reason for the appearance
of two versions of the Mass. The troped version includes the
Gradual *Constitues eos* and the Alleluia verse *Non uos me elegistis*: both are texts long associated with feasts of what might be
called the traditional corps of apostles. For example *Constitues
eos* appears in the Mass for Saint Andrew, and *Alleluia* Y *Non
uos me elegistis* in the Mass for Saints Simon and Juda, both
in Pa 776 (ff.123r and 118r, respectively) and Pa 903 (ff.116r
and 111r, respectively); Pa 780 (f.106) also gives the Gradual for
Saint Andrew's Mass. These responsorial chants are replaced, in

Adémar's untroped Mass for Saint Martial, by *Principes populo-rum* and *Alleluia* ℣ *Beati oculi*, respectively. Both are unique to Pa 909, good circumstantial evidence that they were composed by Adémar himself. Moreover, both melodies are written over erasures that can, to some degree, be read today. The *Alleluia* ℣ *Beati oculi* is one of those copied over an erasure into the libellus of Alleluias elsewhere in the codex, and there too its melody was erased (that is to say, there are two layers of erasures at this point) and replaced with the melody that stands in the untroped Mass. These erasures reveal that the melodies were revised even as Adémar was in the process of executing this formal manuscript. The same pattern of erasure, incidentally, also occurs in the unique Proper tropes for Saint Martial.[20] The only explanation that I find convincing is that Adémar himself is the composer.

With that conclusion in mind we pass to the next issue. Which version of the Mass did Adémar create first? Here a simple codicological observation makes it clear that the troped version, containing the responsorial chants traditionally associated with the apostles, was copied first. The sequence of texts that Adémar wrote on ff.59–85, including the untroped Mass, could not have been started until the new gathering ff.41–48, which transmits the troped Mass, was completed. Only then did he copy the tropes for Saint Benedict for which there was insufficient room in that replacement gathering, as mentioned above. When Adémar came to copy the untroped Mass as part of the cycle of the complete liturgical day, he decided to discard the older responsorial chants and replace them with newly-composed ones. There is a great deal of newly-composed material in the troped Mass, including the other three Proper texts, Introit, Offertory, and Communion, whose sources we shall consider in a moment. These are the three texts that are usually troped, and so, in creating a troped Mass, Adémar devoted more attention to them and simply incorporated two existing, suitable responsorial chants. When he came to write out the untroped Proper texts in full, later in the codex, he took the opportunity to compose two new pieces. In so doing he completely revised the melodies of both pieces after the original newly-composed music had been copied into the manuscript, copied twice in the case of the Alleluia.

Should we, then, discard the older responsories from the troped Mass, or, when considering one version or the other, rigidly observe the distinction that Adémar has made in the manuscript evidence? Either course would, I feel, be too unyielding both to the nature of the document that Adémar created and the exigencies of eleventh-century liturgical observance. Adémar composed a new and splendid liturgy for his Abbey's patron. Nevertheless he has permitted some options, in keeping with a flexible approach to the liturgy whereby some components were left to the discretion of the cantor or performer.[21]

The range of Alleluias provided by Adémar further illuminates this issue. In addition to the Alleluias incorporated into the troped and untroped Masses, Adémar copied a further series of six on ff.61v–62r, and another two on ff.177v–178r, the second of which is a second copy of *Alleluia* Y *Beati oculi*, as noted above: a total of nine discrete Alleluias (see Table 3). Data in this Table are drawn from Karlheinz Schlager's studies of the Alleluia verses, which do not include liturgical assignments for all occurrences of verses and melodies; those assignments given are summarized from his commentary.[22] The Table shows that most of the Alleluias consist of existing verses combined with existing Alleluia melodies, but in unique combinations without concordances in any other medieval source. For example, the verse *Constitues eos* is used in the Masses of apostles and of Saint Luke, but only here in Pa 909 with Schlager's melody 71; this melody, with other verses, is most often found on the feast of a confessor. Three of the verses assigned to Martial by Adémar, *Adnunciauerunt*, *Exaltabuntur*, and *Cum oraret*, are unica, but are used here with melodies familiar from other liturgical applications. Both the verse and the melody of *Beati oculi* are unique and are probably compositions of Adémar himself.

Table 3

Alleluias for Saint Martial in Pa 909

Folios	Verse	Source	Schlager no.	Liturgical Assignment
46r	*Non uos me elegistis*	John 15.16	ThK 79	apostles
61v	*Adnunciauerunt*	Ps. 63.10	ThK 119	only use of this verse melody: martyrs and confessors
61v	*In omnem terram*	Ps. 18.5	ThK 274	verse: St. Matthew, Jacob melody: martyr
62r	*Te gloriosus*		ThK 41	verse: Simon and Jude melody: martyrs
62r	*Exaltabuntur*	Ps. 74.11	ThK 27	only use of this verse melody: Christmas
62r	*Constitues eos*	Ps. 44.17	ThK 71	verse: apostles, St. Luke melody: Confessor
62r	*Cum oraret*		ThK 15	only use of this verse melody: Pentecost
71r	*Beati oculi*		ThK 315	only use of this verse and melody
177v–178r	*Marcialis apostoli*		ThK 27	verse: St. Martial melody: Christmas
178r	*Beati oculi*	(as for f.71r above)		

Only one Alleluia, namely *Marcialis apostolus*, is assigned to Martial's feast in other sources. Adémar draws the pre-existing material, both text and music, from a variety of Masses in the saintly hierarchy, but apostles are well represented among the alleluiatic verses. Adémar's statement is clear: Martial's liturgy is important enough to warrant the creation of new compositions, but at the same time he asserts that the newest apostle is worthy of being honored with pre-existing apostolic texts, as the rubric introducing the Alleluias on f.61v states: *Alleluia de Sancto Marciale uel aliorum apostolorum* ("Alleluia for Saint Martial or of other apostles").

With the other three Proper texts, Introit, Offertory, and Communion, Adémar also blends old and new; but because these texts are conventionally troped in Adémar's period he accords them special attention. All three host texts are newly composed. Clearly the Mass that begins with the Introit *Statuit*, the one traditionally used for Saint Martial, had to be discarded because it was inescapably associated with the status of confessor-bishop. But why should Adémar go to all the trouble of composing new texts when a perfectly good apostolic set existed: the *Mihi autem nimis* Mass? The answer hinges on the fact that Adémar reused many of the existing tropes for Saint Martial and he needed to ensure that the host text fitted around them. This is exactly the reverse of the normal situation, whereby tropes are composed to accommodate an existing text; and yet Adémar's procedure illustrates the importance of tropes within contemporary liturgical practices. Of paramount importance in this regard is the Introit and its attendant tropes. Let us, then, examine the text of the three possible Introits that Adémar could have used to determine their suitability for his needs.

The existing tropes, of course, were created around *Statuit*, the conventional one for Saint Martial's Mass, and completely unsuitable because of its association with the status of confessor-bishop. It is usually divided into four phrases, each of which is preceded by a trope element; *Mihi autem*, however, is most often troped with three elements and so it would be awkward, but not impossible, to use with it existing trope complexes that consist of four elements.[23] A graver difficulty, however, is the literary context of the two Introit texts. *Statuit* opens with a strong statement that God has chosen this man to be His representative and the introductory tropes either amplify this theme or discuss the virtues of the bishop venerated by the feast. On the other hand, the opening phrase of *Mihi autem* states that the friends of God do not receive enough honour. Were the *Statuit* tropes to be sung with *Mihi autem*, the grammatical context would be jarring because the tropes deal with a single person, the honoree of the feast, and *Mihi autem* discusses "friends" in the plural. Example 1 gives the trope *Marcialem prae secla* with both *Statuit* and *Mihi autem*. Here, and in all the examples given below, the host text is printed in capitals.

Example 1
Trope *Marcialem prae secla* with Introits *Statuit* and *Mihi autem*

Marcialem prae secla cunctipotens legit,	*Marcialem prae secla cunctipotens legit,*
nobisque praesulem dedit.	*nobisque praesulem dedit.*
STATVIT EI DOMINVS	MIHI AVTEM NIMIS—
TESTAMENTVM PACIS,	
Quia dignum fore praeuidit, ideoque illum	*Quia dignum fore praeuidit, ideoque illum*
digne ornauit;	*digne ornauit—*
ET PRINCIPEM FECIT EVM,	HONORATI SVNT AMICI TVI, DEVS—
Lemouicam cunctam tanto pastore	*Lemouicam cunctam tanto pastore*
perornans,	*perornans.*
VT SIT ILLI SACERDOCII DIGNITAS.	NIMIS CONFORTATVS EST—
Quam decenter adornans polorum adeptus	*Quam decenter adornans polorum adeptus*
est regna, ubi cum deo regnat	*est regna, ubi cum deo regnat—*
IN ETERNVM.	PRINCIPATVS EORVM.
The All-powerful chose Martial before the	The All-powerful chose Martial before the
generations and gave us a bishop.	generations and gave us a bishop.
HE ESTABLISHED FOR HIM THE	FOR ME, HOWEVER, BEYOND
TESTAMENT OF PEACE,	MEASURE because He foresaw that he
because He foresaw that he would be	would be worthy and therefore he fittingly
worthy and therefore he fittingly prepared	prepared him—
him;	ARE YOUR FRIENDS HONORED,

AND HE MADE HIM THE LEADER, greatly adorning all of Limoges with so great a pastor, SO THAT HE WOULD HAVE THE DIGNITY OF THE PRIESTHOOD. How becomingly he embellishes as he arrives at the kingdoms of the heavens, where he will reign with God FOREVER.	GOD— greatly adorning all of Limoges with so great a pastor. BEYOND MEASURE (how becomingly he embellishes as he arrives at the kingdoms of the heavens, where he will reign with God) IS THEIR DOMINION STRENGTHENED.

Again, it is not impossible to make the latter fit, but certainly the combination with *Statuit* is much smoother. A final consideration, a detailed discussion of which is beyond the scope of this paper, is the modal character of the two Introits. *Statuit* is assigned to mode 1, protus authentic, and *Mihi autem* to mode 2, hence sharing tonality but not modal orientation with *Statuit*. Now tropes often exhibit just this kind of modal ambiguity: invariably their tonality corresponds to that of the host chant, but often their orientation as to authentic or plagal is vague.[24] Hence it is again not impossible to combine tropes composed for a mode 1 chant (*Statuit*) with a mode 2 melody (*Mihi autem*), but once again, not without some awkwardness.

Taken alone, any one of these three difficulties, number of phrases in the text, literary and grammatical context, and musical context, would not, I think, have prevented Adémar from adopting *Mihi autem* for Martial's feast, but the combination of all three would not have permitted a smoothly integrated entity, which was surely Adémar's goal. Therefore he composed an entirely new Introit that would fit with the existing tropes: its melody is clearly mode 1, it can easily be divided into four phrases to accommodate four trope elements, and it opens with a strong statement about God's approval of this man. Example 2 gives the text of *Probauit* with the trope *Marcialem prae secla*, and shows that it provides a much better literary context for the trope than does *Mihi autem*.

Example 2
Trope *Marcialem prae secla* with Introit *Probauit*

Marcialem prae secla cunctipotens legit, nobisque praesulem dedit.
PROBAVIT EVM DEVS ET SCIVIT COR SVVM,
Quia dignum fore praeuidit, ideoque illum digne ornauit.
COGNOVIT SEMITAS SVAS,
Lemouicam cunctam tanto pastore perornans.
DEDVXIT ILLVM IN VIA AETERNA.
Quam decenter adornans polorum adeptus est regna, ubi cum deo regnat,
ET NIMIS CONFORTATVS EST PRINCIPATVS EIVS

The All-powerful chose Martial before the generations and gave us a bishop.
GOD JUDGED HIM AND KNEW HIS HEART,
because He foresaw that he would be worthy and therefore he fittingly prepared him.
HE RECOGNIZED HIS WAY OF LIFE,
greatly adorning all of Limoges with so great a pastor.
HE LED HIM INTO THE ETERNAL WAY.
How becomingly he embellishes as he arrives at the kingdoms of the heavens, where he will reign with God,
AND HIS DOMINION IS STRENGTHENED BEYOND MEASURE.

This same situation obtains with the Offertory, where Adémar reused some of the existing tropes and therefore replaced *Veritas mea* from the episcopal Mass with the newly-composed *Diligo* for the apostolic liturgy.[25] For the Communion, however, Adémar discarded both tropes and host text, and replaced them with newly-composed material. His motivation here, I believe, was that the best-known Communion trope for Martial's feast was *Hic dictis*, a trope that is also used for the feast of Saint Martin, and Adémar was especially anxious to suppress all tropes with this dual allegiance.[26]

Closer study of the Introit *Probauit* and its trope complexes reveals Adémar's technique in blending old and new texts, the paramount importance of this Introit in the new apostolic liturgy, and the contribution of the tropes to that leading role. Let us consider the arrangement of trope complexes, reiterations of the Introit, and indications of the Psalm verses that are to follow the

Introit (see Table 4). Adémar gives a total of ten trope complexes; this total is not overwhelming in the face of the number
presented by Pa 1120 and 1121 in their versions of the Mass for
Saint Martial: eighteen in the former and sixteen in the latter.[27]
What does make Adémar's version staggering is the fact that he
apparently intended all ten complexes to be performed in succession. The evidence for this conclusion is in the indications for
the Psalm verses. Neither Pa 1120 nor 1121 gives any directions
for the placement of Psalm verses or the Doxology, and so in
all likelihood the trope complexes would be used in groups of
three for the usual performance arrangement: IVI●I.[28] Others
were provided in Pa 1120 and 1121 as alternatives or for extra
iterations of the Introit as refrain after a *uersus ad repetendum*
or two.[29] After each of the first nine trope complexes in Pa 909,
however, Adémar furnishes a different Psalm verse, and my conclusion is that he intended all ten complexes to be sung, the tenth
serving as a final refrain after the last Psalm verse.[30] The result
is an introductory piece of extraordinary length. I calculate that
it could take as long as half an hour to perform.[31] I shall return
to the question of this piece's length at the end of the paper; but
it suffices to say here that the tropes constitute an important part
of this piece in both quantity and quality.

Table 4
Tropes for the Introit *Probauit* with Psalm Verses

Plebs deuota	Ps. *Domine probasti me*
Marcialem prae secla	Ps. *Intellexisti*
Marcialis dominum	Ps. *Ecce tu domine*
Inclita refulget	Ps. *Michi autem nimis*
Sedibus externis	Ps. *Hoc est praeceptem*
Marcialem duodenus	Ps. *Vos amici*
Sortis apostolicae	Ps. *Ecce sanctum quem*
Marcialis meritum	Ps. *Iam non dicamus*
Sanctus Marcialis	Ps. *Vos autem dici*
Christi discipulis	

First, however, let us turn to the newly-composed Introit antiphon and the sources of its text (see Example 3).

Example 3
Introit *Probauit* and its Source

Probauit eum deus et sciuit cor suum. cognouit semitas suas; deduxit illum in uia aeterna, et nimis confortatus est principatus eius.	*Ps.* 138.23 **Proba me, deus, et scito cor meum;***interroga me,* **et cognosce semitas meas.** 138.24 *Et uide si uia iniquitatis in me est;* **et deduc me in uia aeterna.** 138.17 *Mihi autem nimis honorificati sunt amici tui deis;* **nimis confortatus est principatus eorum.**

Unlike most such liturgical texts, it is a paraphrase of a Biblical text, here drawn from Psalm 138; in the Example, the phrases borrowed from the Psalm are printed in bold. Also, instead of using a single passage from the Psalm the introit text incorporates phrases from two separate passages. Moreover, the second section of the Psalm from verse 17 is the concluding phrase of the Introit *Mihi autem nimis*, the one usually used for apostles. Thus Adémar integrates a reference to the standard apostolic text in the process of creating a new text that accommodates the existing tropes.

The extent to which that accommodation is made emerges from the pattern of pronouns and possessive adjectives used in the successive phrases of the Introit antiphon. A comparison of the Introit with the pertinent parts of Psalm 138 shows that *Probauit* twice uses the reflexive possessive adjective, *cor suum* and *semitas suas*, in places where neither the grammatical context nor the psalmodic source would suggest it necessary. In both phrases, the reflexive refers not to the subject of the sentence, God the Father, but to the dedicatee of the Introit, Saint Martial. Moreover Martial is also designated by the demonstrative *illum* later in the antiphon. What is the explanation of these unusual usages?

The answer emerges from an editorial policy that I elected at an early stage to use on these texts. That is, I decided to print the text of the troped Introit with the complete text of the antiphon and complete Psalm verses. The result is cumbersome, but it has the advantage of presenting to the modern reader the text as it was heard in performance in the eleventh century. One must also take the trouble to provide meaningful punctuation, but in so doing one must make sense of the text, and here is the chief advantage of the policy, for in combining trope and antiphon, the meaning of this unusual use of reflexive possessive adjectives and demonstrative pronoun is revealed. Example 4 gives the trope *Plebs deuota*, the first in Adémar's series of Introit tropes for Saint Martial's feast, with the antiphon *Probauit*.

Example 4
Trope *Plebs deuota* with Introit *Probauit*

Plebs deuota deo, nostrum nunc suscipe carmen. Nempe uirum colimus de quo sacra
uerba profantur:
PROBAVIT EVM DEVS ET SCIVIT COR SVVM.
Ipse est Marcialis domini praecelsus alumnus—
COGNOVIT SEMITAS SVAS—
Hisraelis quem stirpe deus rex ipse uocauit.
DEDVXIT ILLUM IN VIA AETERNA,
Culmine apostolico clarum quem misit in arua,
ET NIMIS CONFORTATVS EST PRINCIPATVS EIVS.

People devoted to God, now take up our song. Indeed we worship a man concerning
whom the holy words say:
GOD JUDGED HIM AND KNEW HIS HEART.
Marcialis himself is the very lofty pupil of the Lord—
HE RECOGNIZED HIS WAY OF LIFE—
whom God, the King, Himself called from the race of Israel.
HE LED HIM INTO THE ETERNAL WAY,
whom, famous in the apostolic summit, He sent into the fields,
AND HIS DOMINION IS STRENGTHENED BEYOND MEASURE.

Martial appears as the subject of the principle clause of the second trope element, and, because the second and third elements contain subordinate clauses that depend on that principal clause,

Martial remains the subject through the end of the third trope element. In the first three principal clauses of the antiphon, however, God the Father stands as subject of each, and so there is a change of subject with each transition from trope to antiphon and vice versa. Martial also occurs as direct object of the principal clause at the end of the first trope element and as antecedent of the relative pronoun that introduces the subordinate clause that ends this element. Hence Adémar uses the reflexive, or, later, the demonstrative in the antiphon itself to refer back to Martial, subject within the grammatical context of the trope, or, in the first trope element, direct object. This pattern repeats itself throughout the Introit tropes as Martial occurs in prominent grammatical positions in most of the trope elements. (What could be less surprising in liturgical pieces written for his feast?) The reflexive adjectives in the antiphon, then, continue to have a context within which to function. In the case of the first trope complex, *Plebs deuota*, the complete integration of trope and host antiphon is underscored by the fact that Adémar himself composed the last three elements of the trope, namely *Ipse est Marcialis*, *Hisraelis quem stirpe*, and *Culmine apostolo*, thus stressing the notion that the host chant and the trope constitute, in Adémar's mind, a closely united entity.[32]

In short, the antiphon cannot be read or sung by itself and still make grammatical sense. The tropes are obligatory for the literal sense of the antiphon, and this fact makes clear the place of the tropes, particularly Introit tropes, in the new apostolic liturgy. Proper tropes were arguably the preeminent form of devotional expression in early eleventh-century Aquitaine.[33] Adémar expended considerable energy on creating a lavishly troped Mass for Saint Martial and then on integrating it into the existing libellus of Proper tropes in Pa 909. At the same time, the host texts were replaced with new compositions. In particular the Introit was intentionally composed in such a way as to be fully compatible with the existing rich repertory of tropes. This troped version of the Introit requires three and one-quarter folios, more

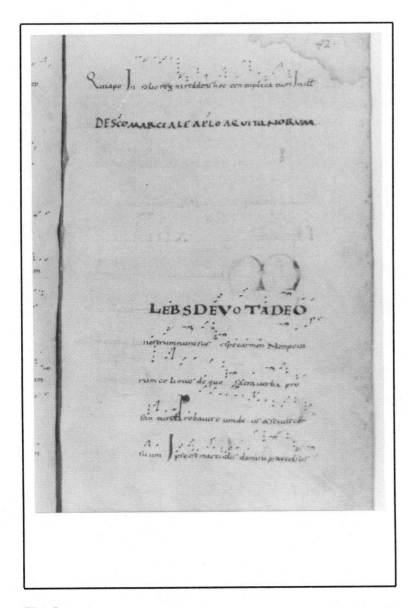

Plate I

Paris, Bibliothèque Nationale, fonds latin, MS 909, f.42r. The opening of the troped mass for the Feast of Saint Martial in the hand of Adémar de Chabannes. Space was left for the initial *P* of *Plebs*; the initial was never executed. Reproduced with the permission of the Département de Manuscrits, Bibliothèque Nationale.

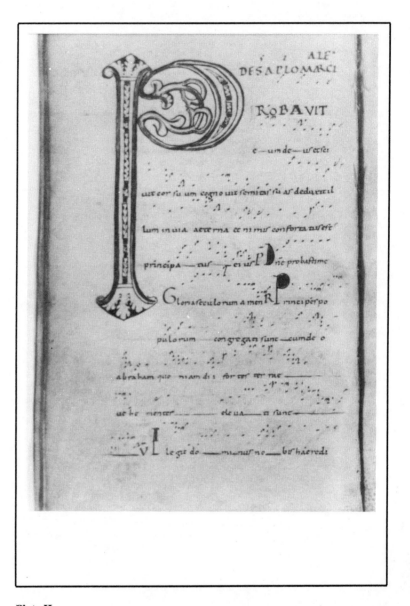

Plate II

Paris, Bibliothèque Nationale, fonds latin, MS 909, f.70v. The opening of the untroped mass for the Feast of Saint Martial in the hand of Adémar de Chabannes. Reproduced with the permission of the Département de Manuscrits, Bibliothèque Nationale.

than any of the nocturns of Matins needs, and would have been introduced by an initial for which nearly half of f.42r was left blank; moreover, it would take about half an hour to sing in its complete form, as mentioned above. Hence, Adémar has created a very special Introit indeed, one that surely accompanied a spectacular liturgical action. And such a grand procession occurred on 3 August 1029, when, according to both of Adémar's reports of the activities of that day, the relics of Saint Martial were displayed in the Cathedral, "his own seat," *sua sedes.*[34]

A standard paradigm for knowledge in the Middle Ages is the image of a dwarf standing on the shoulders of a giant.[35] In his blending of old and new texts, and his renewal of the liturgy for Saint Martial by the careful adaptation of existing texts and skillful insertion of newly-composed ones, Adémar reveals himself to be just such a dwarf, building on the accomplishments of his predecessors. Nevertheless, the very enormity of the project, the proclaiming of a new apostle, the promulgation of a supporting biography, and, perhaps most important, the official recognition of his apostolic status in the liturgy, attest to the audacity and creative originality of Adémar, the monk of Saint Martial.

NOTES

This study is part of a project to edit the complete works of Adémar de Chabannes for the *Corpus Christianorum Continuatio Mediaeualis*, directed by Professor Richard Landes of Boston University. I am grateful to the Principal's Development Fund and the Advisory Research Committee, both of Queen's University, and to the Social Sciences and Humanities Research Council of Canada, for grants that enabled me to consult manuscript sources in Paris and prepare this article for publication. I also thank M. François Avril of the Salle des Manuscrits, Bibliothèque Nationale, and Mme. Contamine of the Section Latine, Institut de Recherche et d'Histoire des Textes, for their many kindnesses.

1. On the date, see Adémar de Chabannes *Epistola de apostolatu sancti Martialis* ed. J.-P. Migne *Patrologiae cursus completus: Series latina [PL]* 141:95–6. Adémar gives the year as 1028, but L. Saltet, "Une discussion sur Saint Martial entre un Lombard et un Limousin

en 1029" *Bulletin de Littérature Ecclésiastique* [*BLE*] 26 (1925) 171
and *n*16, asserts that this is a falsehood. In the proceedings of the
council at Limoges in 1031, Bishop Jordan of Limoges states that the
ceremony took place on the day after the council of 1029 concluded:
edd. P. Labbe and G. Cossart *Sacrosancta concilia* [*Ssc*] (Paris 1671–
72) 9:887–8. These proceedings descend to us only via a copy in
the hand of Adémar de Chabannes, and are probably forgeries; cf.
Saltet "Les faux d'Adémar de Chabannes: Prétendues décisions sur
Saint Martial au concile de Bourges du 1er novembre 1031" *BLE* 27
(1926) 145–6 and *n*6, and "Un cas de mythomanie historique bien
documenté: Adémar de Chabannes (988–1034)" *BLE* 32 (1931) 152–
7. In the proceedings of the council, Jordan specifies that the ceremony
occurred on a Sunday, which statement could be considered additional
verification of the date 1029, as 3 August fell on Sunday that year,
but on Saturday in 1028; see A. Capelli *Cronologia, cronografia e
calendario perpetuo dal principio dell'èra cristiana ai nostri giorni* 5th
ed (Milan 1983) 66–7, 82–3 for 1029 and 1028 respectively. Cf. Saltet
"Une discussion" 170–82.

    2.   Gregory of Tours *Libri octo miraculorum* 8, *Liber in gloria
confessorum* 27–8 ed. B. Krusch **Monumenta Germaniae Historica,
Scriptores Rerum Merouingicarum** [*MGH, SRM*] 1 (Hanover 1885)
764–5; on the date of his mission, see Gregory of Tours *Historia Fran-
corum* 1.30 ed. W. Arndt *MGH, SRM* 1:48. The principal sources for
the episcopal liturgy are: for the Office, Paris: Bibliothèque Nationale,
fonds latin [Pa], MS 1253 ff.15–21, Pa 1085 ff.76v–77r (a breviary
and antiphoner, respectively, both from the early eleventh century),
and, for the Mass, Pa 1120 ff.46–51, Pa 1121 ff.28v–32r (both tropers
from the early eleventh century). See also J. Chailley *L'école musicale de Saint Martial de Limoges jusqu'à la fin du XIe siècle* (Paris
1960) 62–3; P. Evans *The Early Trope Repertory of Saint Martial de
Limoges* **Princeton Studies in Music** 2 (Princeton 1970) 44–5; J. Grier
"*Ecce sanctum quem deus elegit Marcialem apostolum*: Adémar de
Chabannes and the Tropes for the Feast of Saint Martial" *Beyond the
Moon: Festschrift Luther Dittmer* edd. B. Gillingham and P. Merkley
Wissenschaftliche Abhandlungen 53 (Ottawa 1990) 36–47.

    3.   On Saint Martial as a pilgrimage destination, see C. de Lasteyrie
*L'abbaye de Saint-Martial de Limoges: Étude historique, économique
et archéologique précédée de recherches nouvelles sur la vie du saint*
(Paris 1901) 31–41; B. Töpfer "Reliquienkult und Pilgerbewegung zur

Zeit der Klosterreform im burgundisch-aquitanischen Gebiet" *Vom Mittelalter zur Neuzeit: Zum 65. Geburtstag von Heinrich Sproemberg* ed. H. Kretzschmar **Forschungen zur mittelalterlichen Geschichte** 1 (Berlin 1956) 420–39, esp. 428–33; D. F. Callahan "The Sermons of Adémar de Chabannes and the Cult of St. Martial of Limoges" *Revue Bénédictine* 86 (1976) 253–5, 280–95; R. Landes "The Making of a Medieval Historian: Ademar de Chabannes and Aquitaine at the Turn of the Millennium" (Ph.D. diss. Princeton 1984) 60–80.

4.   A series of gifts from Bishop Jordan and his family to the Abbey of Saint Martial, one of which acknowledges the Saint as an apostle, attests to the donor's positive attitude towards the Abbey: *Premier cartulaire de l'aumonerie de S. Martial* no. 28, 30, 32–34, 36, *Second cartulaire de l'aumonerie de S. Martial* no. 34 and 35 edd. A. Leroux, E. Molinier, and A. Thomas **Documents historiques baslatins, provençaux et français concernant principalement la Marche et le Limousin** (Limoges 1883–85) 2:10–15, 20–1. Of these, no. 32, names Saint Martial as an apostle. For commentary on these documents and on the attitude of the cathedral canons, see J. Becquet "Les évêques de Limoges aux Xe, XIe et XIIe siècles" *Bulletin de la Société Archéologique et Historique du Limousin [BSAHL]* 105 (1978) 99–101, 104; cf. Lasteyrie *L'abbaye* 75–9; Saltet "Une discussion" 171–3.

5.   The feast is identified in the proceedings of the council at Limoges in 1031: edd. Labbe and Cossart *Ssc* 9:888. Cf. [F.] Arbellot "Cathédrale de Limoges: Histoire et description" *BSAHL* 3 (1848) 171–2; Saltet "Une discussion" 173.

6.   On Adémar's biography, see L. Delisle "Notice sur les manuscrits originaux d'Adémar de Chabannes" *Notices et extraits des manuscrits de la Bibliothèque Nationale et autres bibliothèques* 35 (Paris 1896) 241–358; Saltet "Une discussion" 161–86, 279–302, "Une prétendue lettre de Jean XIX sur Saint Martial fabriquée par Adémar de Chabannes" *BLE* 27 (1926) 117–39, "Les faux" 145–60, "Un cas de mythomanie" 149–65; Callahan "The Sermons" 251–95, "Adémar de Chabannes et la Paix de Dieu" *Annales du Midi* 89 (1977) 21–43; R. L. Wolff "How the News was brought from Byzantium to Angoulême; or, The Pursuit of a Hare in an Ox Cart" *Byzantine and Modern Greek Studies* 4 (1978) 139–89; R. Landes "The Making of a Medieval Historian." For further bibliography, see Grier *"Ecce sanctum"* 28 *n*2.

7. Chailley mentions the appearance of a second hand in this codex, "Les anciens tropaires et séquentiaires de l'école de Saint-Martial de Limoges (Xe–XIe s.)" *Études Grégoriennes* 2 (1957) 174–5, and makes a tentative attribution to Adémar, *L'école* 88–91. H. Husmann, *Tropen- und Sequenzenhandschriften* **Répertoire International des Sources Musicales** B 5:1 (Munich 1964) 119, and Evans, *The Early Trope Repertory* 49, both mention the intrusion without alluding to Adémar. Only J. A. Emerson unequivocally attributes this gathering to Adémar: "Two Newly Identified Offices for Saints Valeria and Austriclinianus by Adémar de Chabannes (MS Paris, Bibl. Nat., Latin 909, FOLS. 79–85v)" *Speculum* 40 (1965) 33–5; cf. Grier *"Ecce sanctum"* 35–40.

8. The letter appears in autograph in Pa 5288 ff.51–59, and is published in *PL* 141:89–112. A new edition will appear in the forthcoming edition of Adémar's collected works in **Corpus Christianorum Continuatio Mediaeualis**. For commentary, see Saltet "Une discussion."

9. Chailley "Les anciens tropaires" 176–7, *L'école* 90–1; Husmann *Tropen* 119. On the restoration of 1979, see M. Huglo "On the Origins of the Troper-Proser" *Journal of the Plainsong & Medieval Music Society* 2 (1979) 17, 18 *n*27 (trans. of "Aux origines du Tropaire-Prosaire" *Nordiskt kollokvium i latinsk liturgiforskning* 3 [Oslo 1978] 53–65).

10. On the influence of the tropers Pa 1120 and 1121, both of the Abbey of Saint Martial, and the book's intended use at the Abbey of Saint Martin, see Grier *"Ecce sanctum"* 54–69. Chailley, "Les anciens tropaires" 174 and *L'école* 90, assigns the manuscript to Saint Martin. Most scholars attribute Pa 909 to Saint Martial, e.g., Husmann *Tropen* 118–9. A tantalizing piece of evidence is provided by the appearance of a troped Mass for Saint Androchius in the hand of the first scribe (ff.58–59r, directly following that for Saint Valery, whose feast falls on 10 December). This shadowy saint appears in liturgical manuscripts associated with Saint Martial: in the Kalendar of Pa 1240 (f.14r), which gives his feast as 6 August; and in the sacramentary Pa 821 f.72v (but not its Kalendar), where his feast is combined with that of Saints Felicissimus and Agapitus, companions of Saint Sixtus, the third-century pope, also on 6 August. There is also a tenuous link between Androchius and Saint Martin, in that it was reported that the saint's body was carried to Saint Martin on 4 April 1520 (Pa 5239 f.21r; printed in H. Duplès-Agier, ed. *Chroniques de Saint-Martial de*

Limoges [Paris 1874] 215). Further on Saint Androchius, see R. Jacobsson "Contribution à la géographie des saints" *La traditizione dei tropi liturgici* edd. C. Leonardi and E. Menesto (Spoleto 1990) 168–76.

11. Chailley "Les anciens tropaires" 175, *L'école* 89; D. Gaborit-Chopin *La décoration des manuscrits à Saint-Martial de Limoges et en Limousin du IXe au XIIe siécle Mémoires et Documents Publiés par la Société de l'école de Chartres* 17 (Paris and Geneva 1969) 183; Evans *The Early Trope Repertory* 32–3; Grier "*Ecce sanctum*" 35.

12. Grier "*Ecce sanctum*" 36–7.

13. Grier "*Ecce sanctum*" 66.

14. Chailley "Les anciens tropaires" 176, *L'école* 88–91; Emerson "Two Newly Identified Offices" 33–5; Gaborit-Chopin *La décoration* 183; Wolff "How the News was brought" 153, 173.

15. P. Hooreman "Saint-Martial de Limoges au temps de l'Abbé Odolric (1025–1040): Essai sur une pièce oubliée du répertoire limousin" *Revue Belge de Musicologie* 3 (1949) 16–30; he also notes that other parts of Pa 909 are in Adémar's hand without specifying which folios. On the sequentiary and its extension, see also Chailley "Les anciens tropaires" 176–7, *L'école* 91; Husmann *Tropen* 119; J. Vezin "Un nouveau manuscrit d'Adémar de Chabannes (Paris, Bibl. nat., lat.7231)" *Bulletin de la Société Nationale des Antiquaires de France* (Paris 1965) 45; Gaborit-Chopin *La décoration* 183; Wolff "How the News was brought" 152–3; Huglo "Codicologie et musicologie" *Miscellanea codicologica F. Masai dicata MCMLXXIX*, edd. P. Cockshaw, M.-C. Garand, and P. Jodogne *Les Publications de Scriptorium* 8 (Gand 1979) 1:76–81, esp. 79–80, and "On the Origins" 14.

16. Alleluias: ff.177v–178r. Processional antiphon: f.251r. Tonary: ff.251–257; cf. Huglo *Les tonaires: Inventaire, analyse, comparaison Publications de la Société Française de Musicologie* 3/2 (Paris 1971), 154 *n*3, who notes erasures on f.255.

17. Delisle "Les manuscrits de Saint-Martial de Limoges: Réimpression textuelle du Catalogue publié en 1730" *BSAHL* 43 (1895) 4, "Notice" 350–2; Huglo, "Codicologie et musicologie" 80.

18. On the office for Sainte Foy, see Chailley "Les anciens tropaires" 166; Huglo "Codicologie et musicologie" 74 *n*17. In the liturgy for Saint Géraud d'Aurillac, see A. E. Planchart "Fragments, Palimpsests, and Marginalia" *Journal of Musicology* 6 (1988) 297–305, who also identifies two other such examples in non-Aquitanian manuscripts.

19. I am indebted to Illo Humphrey for identifying *Marcialem apostolum Petrus* as a Tract.

20. Grier "*Ecce sanctum*" 47–50.

21. On the role of the cantor, see M. E. Fassler "The Office of the Cantor in Early Western Monastic Rules and Customaries: A Preliminary Investigation" *Early Music History* 5 (1985) 29–51, esp. 46–51.

22. K.-H. Schlager *Thematischer Katalog der ältesten Alleluia-Melodien aus Handschriften des 10. und 11. Jahrhunderts, ausgenommen das ambrosianische, alt-römische und alt-spanische Repertoire Erlanger Arbeiten zur Musikwissenschaft* 2 (Munich 1965), ed. *Alleluia Melodien* (1 *bis 1100*) **Monumenta Monodica Medii Aeui** [*MMMA*] 7 (Kassel and Basel 1968).

23. See the trope complexes given for *Mihi autem* in G. Weiß ed. *Introitus-tropen* (1 *Das Repertoire der südfranzösischen Tropare des 10. und 11. Jahrhunderts MMMA* 3 (Kassel and Basel 1970) 153–62 no. 130–140. Only one trope complex, no. 139, consists of four elements, whereas as many as four contain only two (no. 131, 132, 126, 140). Further on the composition of new Propers for the apostolic liturgy for Saint Martial and their relationship to the tropes, see R.M. Jacobsson "Att tillverka en apostel: Bibliotekhistoria och hagiografi" *Bibliotek: Tradition och utveckling—Festschrift till Lars-Erik Sanner den 18 januari 1991* (Stockholm 1991) 250–9.

24. See Evans *The Early Trope Repertory* 86–7; Grier "*Ecce sanctum*" 50–3.

25. On the question of the relation between trope and host text and chant, see Evans *The Early Trope Repertory* 55–118; A. Dennery *Le chant postgrégorien: Tropes, séquences et prosules Musique—Musicologie* 19 (Paris 1989) 112–9.

26. The following manuscripts place *Hic dictis* in the Mass for Saint Martin: Pa 1120 ff.63v–64r, Pa 1121 f.41v, Pa 909 f.57r, Pa 1119 f.78r, Pa 1118 f.98v, Pa 887 f.42r, Pa 1084 f.88v, Pa 1871 f.36v, Pa 779 f.115r, Pa 903 f.161r. Two manuscripts, written at Saint Martial, also place it in the Mass of Saint Martial: Pa 1120 f.51v, Pa 1121 f.41v. On the suppression of tropes that share assignment to both Saints Martin and Martial, see Grier "*Ecce sanctum*" 57–64.

27. Pa 1120 ff.46–50v; one further complex is presented on f.63r. Pa 1121 ff.28v–32r.

28. A. Hughes *Medieval Manuscripts for Mass and Office: A Guide to Their Organization and Terminology* (Toronto 1982) 34–5;

see xvii–xix and endpapers for the abbreviations. On the grouping of trope complexes in threes, see Planchart *The Repertory of Tropes at Winchester* (Princeton 1977) 1:69–78.

29. Planchart *The Repertory* 1:69–78; Hughes *Medieval Manuscripts* 34–5.

30. For more detailed discussion of this arrangement and the omission by Adémar of the Doxology, see Grier *"Ecce sanctum"* 41–4.

31. My calculation is based on the performance of a troped version of the Easter Introit *Resurrexi et adhuc* on the recording *Anglo-Saxon Easter*, Schola Gregoriana of Cambridge, directed by Mary Berry, Archiv 413 546–1 (Hamburg 1984). Four troped iterations of the Introit are sung in the arrangement IVI●IVI (i.e., one *uersus ad repetendum* is used), and the entire piece takes 11' 50".

32. On Adémar's original compositions in the troped Mass, see Grier *"Ecce sanctum"* 38–40, 47–54.

33. Evans *The Early Trope Repertory* 4–6; Huglo "La tradition musicale aquitaine: Répertoire et notation" *Liturgie et musique (IXe–XIVe s.), Cahiers de Fanjeaux* 17 (Toulouse 1982) 257, Table 2; Grier *"Ecce sanctum"* 32–4.

34. *Epistola de apostolum Martialis* in *PL* 141:92; proceedings of the council of 1031, edd. Labbe and Cossart *Ssc* 9:888–9.

35. This statement appears to be a *locus communis* in the twelfth century: William of Conches, Glosses on Priscian, in E. Jeauneau "Deux rédactions des gloses de Guillaume de Conches sur Priscien" *Recherches de théologie Ancienne et Médiévale* 27 (1960) 234–6, text on 235; John of Salisbury, *Metalogicon* 3.4 ed. C. C. I. Webb (Oxford 1929) 136, attributes the saying to Bernard of Chartres; A. Neckam *De naturis rerum* 1.78 ed. T. Wright *Rerum Britannicarum Medii Aeui (Rolls Series)* 34 (London 1863) 123, gives as his source, *philosophus*, who in this instance seems not to be Aristotle. For other sources and commentary, see E. Jeauneau "Nains et géants" *Entretiens sur la renaissance du 12e siècle* edd. M. de Gandillac and E. Jeauneau *Decades du Centre Culturel International de Cérisy-la-Salle* n.s. 9 (Paris 1968) 21–52, who believes (31–5) that Bernard of Chartres is the source for this remark.

Editing and Translating
Medieval Arabic Writings on Music

George Dimitri Sawa
Centre for Studies in Middle Eastern Music

In this paper I discuss editorial problems I encountered while working on my Canada Research Fellowship project, *Source Readings in Medieval Middle Eastern Music History.* Intended as a supplement to Oliver Strunk's *Source Readings in Music History,* the project draws on two types of discourse under the general rubric of music theory and music literature, and it covers a historical period from about 750 to 1450 AD. Below there follows a summary of the project.

Part One: Music Literature

1) Physical Setting and Format of Music Making
2) Uses and Functions of Songs
3) Concept of Music
4) Behavior: physical/verbal/social
5) Learning and Oral Transmission
6) Women Musicians
7) Nature and Process of Musical and Textual Change

Part Two: Music Theory

1) Concept of Rhythm, Rhythmic Modes, Meters and Tempi
2) Tone Systems and Modes
3) Melodic, Harmonic, and Timbral Ornamentation Techniques
4) Nature of Preludes and Postludes
5) Instruments and Instrumental Music

SOURCES AND TOOLS. Whereas sources on music theory are limited in number, and tend to focus on the subject of theory, the sources on music literature are enormous in sheer volume, and prove difficult to delimit because of the variety of literary genres in which they appear. The latter include: *belles-lettres*, anthologies, anecdotal writings, entertaining works in general, collections of songs and poems, books on singers, instrumentalists, races, and women, essays on love and passion, histories (economic, social, cultural, intellectual, political, and military), geographies, travellers' accounts, Islamic law and *samā'* (admissibility or non-admissibility of listening to music), books on proverbs, works on zoology and cosmology.[1]

Even when edited, theoretical and literary sources are most often not indexed, and if indexed, they either lack subject indices altogether or have indices that omit subjects that concern musicologists. For their work on sources of both theory and literature, researchers have at their disposal an array of tools, including medieval biographies, bibliographies, dictionaries, encyclopedias, treatises on grammar, prosody, rhetoric, mathematics, logic, and the fine arts.[2]

ON THE USEFULNESS OF TRANSLATION. People often ask me, "Why translate into English?" or "Why not simply edit and benefit the Arab reader interested in medieval Middle Eastern music?"

One reason may be that I come from a family of professional translators and, in a sense, inherited a family business.[3] Another reason may be construed as a practical one: I live in Canada, taught at the University of Toronto, where the main language of instruction is English, and as a researcher enjoyed the patronage of the Social Sciences and Humanities Research Council of Canada and the University. A third and more important reason concerns the dissemination of knowledge about this little known subject on a wide scale to many scholars, among them: Western musicologists interested in the interchange between Europe and the Middle East in theoretical and practical matters; specialists in ancient Greek music interested in knowing how Middle Eastern theorists (e.g., al-Fārābī and Avicenna) understood and interpreted ancient Greek theorists (e.g., Euclid and Ptolemy); ethnomusicologists and anthropologists interested in musical theories and concepts as articulated in Arabic medieval sources, and the possible applicability of such theories and concepts to contemporary Middle Eastern music or to world musics in general; scholars of Middle Eastern social and cultural history who tend to see Middle Eastern music solely as theory or as a performing art. Because such scholars are often intimidated by the technical nature of the subject, they are unaware that much music literature belongs to their own field of expertise, be it social or literary history. A fourth reason, and I speak as a native translating from his mother tongue (Arabic) into a second language (English), is that the unsaid must become said, the implicit must become explicit, and meanings hidden in the unconscious must through the rigorous process of translation become conscious. This is usually the case with translating from Arabic when one deals with issues that pertain to morphology and semantics in the painful quest of *le mot juste*.

LE MOT JUSTE AND ITS EDITORIAL IMPLICATIONS. (a) *Le mot juste*. It is more the exception than the rule. For example, the English "rhythmic mode" or "rhythmic cycle" is *le mot juste* to translate the Arabic word *dawr*, and similarly, the English "attack" to translate the Arabic word *naqra*. For the sake of editorial consistency, the first time *le mot juste* appears, it is accompanied by its Arabic counterpart in italics and in brackets; e.g., rhythmic cycle *(dawr)*. Thereafter I use only the English word. Both the transliterated Arabic word and its English translation appear in a glossary of technical terms and of course in the index. The transliterated Arabic word in both the glossary and index has a cross-reference; e.g., *dawr:* see rhythmic cycle. (b) No *mot juste*. This problem occurs with technical words that have no equivalent in English. Such words are best left in transliterated form; e.g., the rhythmic mode known as the *ramal* (see Examples 1 and 2 below). In such cases the words should be defined briefly in the glossary and simply entered in the index. (c) *Les mots justes*. When translating from Arabic to English, one often encounters the problem of English words whose meaning is insufficient to translate an Arabic word.[4] In these cases two or more words should be used in juxtaposition to convey the intended meaning; e g., the word *nuḥṣī* in Example 1. (d) Short of *le mot juste*. An equivalent English word can be used to convey the intended and the general meaning of an Arabic word. The English word will appear in italics before the Arabic word in italics and in brackets. But stopping at this point may rob the reader of the deeper meanings and concepts buried in complex Arabic words. To remedy this gap, a footnote should be added in order to provide the nuances of such words (e.g., *rasm, tuḍāribunī, rawm,* and *ishmām* in Examples 1, 3, and 8). This problem becomes more acute when we consider the structure of the Arabic language: a word not only has many meanings by itself, but it also acquires additional meanings because of morphological/semantic exigencies[5] (e.g., the word *masha* in Example 3).

TRANSLITERATION OF ARABIC SCRIPT. A decision must be made as to what should be transliterated as opposed to translated,[6] and what should be left in Arabic script. Matters of interest to Middle Eastern specialists, but not to Western readers, should remain in Arabic (e.g., Example 3). Further, a copyist's error may make little sense in transliteration, but a great deal of sense in Arabic script. This is especially true in the case of dots over or under Arabic letters, or when one letter is mistaken for another because the two are orthographically close, though not so phonetically (e.g., Example 7), or when a passage involves morphologies of a word that are clear only in Arabic script.[7]

PRELUDES, INTERLUDES, AND POSTLUDES. The above editorial problems concern the translation of a word, regardless of whether this word occurs in a short passage or in a long treatise. In the latter case, the editor should supply a detailed commentary (to function as a prelude or preface), editorial additions about implied meanings in square brackets in the text (the interludes, so to speak), and perhaps some concluding remarks (a postlude) in cases where preludes and interludes do not suffice.

This process of "preluding," "interluding," and "postluding" is even more crucial for short passages; for instance, anecdotes from *Kitāb al-Aghānī (Book of Songs)* that are replete with information so subtle as to pass unnoticed by a non-expert in Middle Eastern historical and cultural history (see Examples 8 and 9).

SORTING AND ARRANGING THE MATERIAL. Theoretical writings on music tend to be more disciplined and narrow in focus in comparison with literary writings on music, especially the anecdotal type. When arranging a collection of sources, editors may often be at a loss as to where to place a specific anecdote. For instance, Example 8 could be included under "Behavior," "Women Musicians," or "Learning and Oral Transmission."

PRIMARY AND SECONDARY SOURCES. Whenever possible I have used primary sources, that is, the manuscripts themselves. Otherwise, I have relied on microfilm copies. Editions and previous translations, if carefully and faithfully executed, can be very useful. When the latter have been done carelessly, they prove to be a nuisance, for they must be cited along with justification for corrections and differing interpretations. The problems I face in preparing my anthology do not concern what I see as clear-cut cases of mistranslation, misunderstanding, or editorial licence, but rather the degree of tolerance to be shown towards infidelity in translating texts (e.g., Examples 4 and 5).

To illustrate the above points, I shall use the works of two tenth-century scholars: the *Grand Book of Music*, and the *Book for the Basic Comprehension of Rhythms* by the music theorist Abū Naṣr al-Fārābī (d.950), and the *Book of Songs* by the music *littérateur* Abū al-Faraj al-Iṣbahānī (d.967). The first was born in Transoxiana, and came to Baghdād to study philosophy, logic, grammar, mathematics, prosody, and rhetoric. Known primarily as a logician (he was named the "second master," Aristotle being the "first") and a political philosopher, al-Fārābī is nonetheless a music theorist of genius, whose work remains unsurpassed in the field of Middle Eastern music theory. His *Grand Book of Music* deals with both ancient Greek and medieval Middle Eastern music. His *Book for the Basic Comprehension of Rhythms*[8] is a revision of the theory of rhythms expounded in the *Grand Book*. Basing his theory on empirical evidence provided by the repertory of his time, al-Fārābī transcribes for us many examples of the rhythmic modes in their fundamental and embellished forms.

The second writer, al-Iṣbahānī, was born in Iṣfahān. He also came to Baghdād to study historiography, *belles-lettres*, poetry, prosody, and grammar. It took him fifty years to compile his *Book of Songs*. The modern edition of this work comprises twenty-four volumes—roughly ten thousand pages of concise medieval Arabic. The *Book of Songs* describes in anecdotal fashion the poetical and musical events that took place from the sixth to the tenth century in the cities of Makka, al-Madīna, Damascus, and Baghdād. His sources include oral and written histories, and even letters between musicians, all cross-checked, cross-referenced, and collated. The *Book of Songs* is indeed a remarkable achievement in music ethnography.

Example 1
Al-Fārābī, *Kitāb Iḥṣā' al-Īqā'āt*
(Book for the Basic Comprehension of Rhythms)
Manisa Public Library, Ms 1705 f.59b[9]

This passage was chosen to illustrate problems associated with *le mot juste:* specifically (b) No *mot juste*, (c) *Les mots justes*, and (d) Short of *le mot juste*. The notes are intended to clarify layers of meanings and concepts, and in this respect, the passage shows how useful encyclopedias and dictionaries can be. The square brackets in the text (interludes) lessen the number of notes required, and thus facilitate reading.

In the name of God, the Merciful, the Compassionate, God ease [my task].

We have aimed in this book to enumerate, classify, and attain a basic comprehension[10] of the species of *īqā'āt;*[11] and to cause them to exist for the first time *(nakhtari'uhā)* by means of notation *(rasm);*[12] and to bring about what we know of their state [of being], using the approach of a follow-up [over portions of previous studies[13]] only; and to [further] confine ourselves when (correcting) what we are narrowly focusing on, to examining it by means of [our] sensory perceptions and by seeking evidence from what appears in practice in the arts whose concern is the use of the *īqā'*.[14] And we shall use in our discourse[15] the old name [of an *īqā'*] when it has an old name, and for that which no name has reached us from our predecessors, we shall "transfer" to it a name of the closest of things resembling it.[16]

Example 2
Al-Fārābī, *Kitāb Iḥṣā' al-Īqā'āt*
(Book for the Basic Comprehension of Rhythms)
Manisa f.64a

In this passage I demonstrate the use of brackets in the text for editorial additions designed to reduce the number of notes and to facilitate reading. The example is the first appearance in the manuscript of the final and improved notational system for rhythms: it contains explanatory captions beneath the component parts of the *īqāʿ*, and also exhibits alphabetic notation, phonetics, as well as diacritical, geometrical, and arithmetical signs. The Arabic shows the transcription as a "drawing" of considerable artistic quality.[17] Under the translated captions I have supplied two types of transcription: one quite close to the spirit of al-Fārābī's notation, with downward arrows to indicate timeless attacks separated one from the other by durations; the other a standard Western method for easy understanding of the rhythmic mode. The captions indicating the first and second cycles are translations of the text proper.

[The *Heavy-Ramal*, Notation of *Fundamental*]

The first among the *heavy [īqāʿāt]*[18] is the *heavy-ramal*.[19] [As has been said], its cycles in their *fundamental* form follow one another two attacks, two attacks, etc. Let us place between every two attacks present in the cycles [of the *fundamental* the sign of] the *medium* time [unit (o)], and between every two cycles [the sign of] the double time [unit (oo)], and let that way of writing be a law *(qānūn)* to follow in whatever we show in the category of the *heavy-heavy-īqāʿāt*. [See Figure 1]

Example 3
Al-Fārābī, *Grand Book of Music*[20]

This passage shows not only the importance of phonological, grammatical, and lexical tools, but also the problems related to cases of (a) *Le mot juste* as well as (d) Short of *le mot juste* with its accompanying note. Arabic script has been used whenever a term is important to specialists in the Middle East, but inconsequential to musicologists. However, transliteration is used whenever a word becomes the focus of a discussion in a note.

[Types of Attacks: Dynamics and Timbral Properties]

Let the extremities of the durations of the *īqāʿāt* be delimited by means of attacks, and let us postulate the attacks as belonging to three classes: some are loud (قوية) ; some are soft

(لِينة) ; and some are moderate (مُتوسّطة) . The loud resembles the *nunnation* (تَنوِين) : the desinential inflection in
the grammar of the Arabic language;[21] the moderate resembles
the [short] vowel[s] (حركة) added to the letter[s] (حرف) in
that language;[22] and the soft resembles the *scent (ishmām)* or
the *slurring (rawm)* of the vowel.[23] Some people give (يوقع)
the name attack *(naqra)* to those [attacks] which are loud and
complete (تام) only; as for the moderate [attack], they call it
a *rubbing (masha)* [24] and the soft [they call] a *wink (ghamza)*.
It is better to "transfer" (تنقل) to them those [technical] terms
used to denote phonemes[25] (حروف) that resemble the corresponding sounds of the attacks. And these terms are taken from
the grammarians of every language. As for us, we shall "transfer" to the attacks [to indicate their sounds, corresponding sound
of phonemes defined by] terms used by the grammarians of the
Arabic language. Thus let us name the soft by the term *slurring
(rawm)*, and the moderate by the term *scent (ishmām)*.[26]

Example 4
Al-Fārābī, *Grand Book of Music*[27]

I have chosen this short passage to demonstrate the kind of infidelity, found in a French translation, which I believe should be
challenged. The French version by Rodolphe d'Erlanger, shown
below, gives the gist of the passage, but robs the reader of the
subtle nuances of the original. For instance, the word *fixer* is
incorrect, because al-Fārābī was speaking more precisely about
notation or transcription; therefore I used the word "notated."
Likewise, the word *temps* is incorrect, because al-Fārābī was
explaining musical tempo in terms of visual notation, that is to
say, the temporal in terms of the spatial; therefore I used the
word "distance." What al-Fārābī means to say is that the more
space there is between the attacks, the longer the duration and
the slower the tempo. This intriguing piece of information is lost
unless the translation captures the sense of the original passage,
a goal which I have attempted to achieve in the English version,
also below.

Figure 1

taṅ	[o]	taṅ	o	o	taṅ	o	taṅ	[o]	[o]
its first *medium-heavy* attack	*medium* time unit	[its second *medium-heavy* attack]	[*medium* time unit]	[*medium* time unit]	[its first *medium-heavy* attack]	*medium* time unit	[its second *medium-heavy* attack]	[*medium* time unit]	[*medium* time unit]

first cycle ——————— *second cycle* ———————

The zero signs represent the value of the separator, which is by definition worth double the time unit of the cycle.

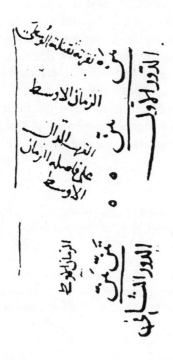

Nous pouvons raccourcir ou rallonger les temps qui séparent les
percussions des rythmes disjoints que nous venons de fixer, . . .

And it is possible to make closer [the durational] distance between the attacks of these species of *disjunctives* herein notated
(ست.مَت‎) , or to lengthen the distance between them, . . .

Example 5
Al-Fārābī, *Grand Book of Music*[28]

In this passage the infidelity in d'Erlanger's French translation
consists of an impersonal construction that omits the performer
as actor (although he or she is implied, as are his or her actions).
Most important, this version does not do justice to al-Fārābī's
thinking. Because al-Fārābī sees the performer essentially as a
"mover" of notes, it is precisely the concepts of the "mover"
and the "moving" of notes that lie at the heart of the subject
of rhythms. The two versions given below illustrate the difference between a loose paraphrase and a more exact replication of
meaning.

Introduites dans le dernier cycle d'une mélodie, les percussions
supplémentaires jouent le rôle de points d'appui et facilitent l'ar-
rêt de l'évolution.

As for the attacks used in the last cycle of a melody, they
are used as *supports (i'timādāt,* plural of *i'timād),* enabling the
mover to rely upon them to cut off the *motion* [of notes].

Example 6
Al-Fārābī, *Grand Book of Music*[29]

This passage demonstrates the kind of infidelity I find acceptable.
It can be justified on the grounds that it avoids redundancy, and
yet does not leave out any important nuances of the original text.
For purposes of comparison I give below two versions, the first
a literal translation, the second a shorter version of the passage.

Thus the *[temporal] gradation*[30] keeps intact the duration of the melody as a whole and does not shorten it; whereas the *acceleration* changes the duration of the melody as a whole and causes it to be smaller.

Thus the *[temporal] gradation* neither changes nor shortens the duration of the melody as a whole; whereas the *acceleration* shortens it.

Example 7
Al-Fārābī, *Grand Book of Music*[31]

The note used for this passage shows the usefulness of including the Arabic script in order to clarify copyists' mistakes. The word (البهاء) *al-bahā'*, which means "brilliancy," has been copied wrongly as (النقاء) *naqā'*, which means "purity." The Arabic orthography demonstrates in a way impossible in a transliteration how the misplacement of a simple dot (from bottom to top) and the misreading of one letter could have confused a copyist.

As for the *conjunctive [īqā'āt]*, they have little brilliancy *(bahā')*[32] because of the equality of their durations, and, as a result, something resembling boredom overtakes the soul *(nafs)*, and the rhythmic order of the notes of the melodies is less satisfactory.

Example 8
Al-Iṣbahānī, *Kitāb al-Aghānī (Book of Songs)*
Cairo 1923–74 6:261

In this anecdotal passage we see the crucial importance of some of the tools mentioned earlier for interpreting the anecdote and framing it with the proper historical and social context. The tools include biographical/bibliographical dictionaries, regular language dictionaries, grammatical treatises, and social and economic histories. The commentary that precedes the passage is an example of a "prelude" that offers the reader useful preliminary information. Though some words are left in Arabic script for the benefit of Middle Eastern experts, others are transliterated, since their morphological and semantic aspects are discussed in detailed notes.

COMMENTARY. The following anecdote is a priceless piece of information on music education: the method of oral transmission is one to one, and the learning process is arduous and repetitive, requiring the student to imitate the master's example. The length of apprenticeship is stated here as seven years of daily lute lessons, and the financial gains of a music educator point to a rather lucrative profession. The teacher was paid thirty thousand dirhams over the seven-year period, that is, about three hundred and fifty dirhams per month. This sum exceeds by fifty dirhams the amount needed for a middle-class family to live decently at that time.[33] The chain of transmission of the story seems quite sound in this case: a short chain of three narrators, two of them father and son, to a third, the writer al-Iṣbahānī.

I was informed by Muḥammad ibn Mazyad,[34] on the authority of Ḥammād ibn Isḥāq,[35] on the authority of his father [Isḥāq al-Mawṣilī], who one day recalled (ذكر) 'Ātika bint Shuhda[36] and said:

> On the 'ūd, she was the best performer (أضرب) [37]
> I have seen. I spent seven years going to her every day,
> and she taught me [the playing of the 'ūd (tuḍāribunī),[38]
> and the lesson consisted of] one or two pieces (ḍarb)[39]
> [a day]. She received from me and my father [Ibrāhīm
> al-Mawṣilī] more than thirty thousand dirhams for my
> lessons: [the payments were] in dirhams and gifts.[40]

Example 9
Al-Iṣbahānī, *Book of Songs* Cairo 6:184

Like Example 8, this passage requires the use of such tools as dictionaries, treatises, and other types of secondary sources. The anecdote contains an obscene proverb that needs a lengthy explanation, which is inserted as an interlude.[41]

COMMENTARY. In this anecdote the chain of transmission is strong: the story about the singer-prince Ibrāhīm ibn al-Mahdī (d.224/839) is told to his son Hibat-Allāh (d.275/888) by two of the prince's singing slave-girls, Rayyiq and Shāriya,[42] who witnessed the event itself. Hibat-Allāh, the son of Ibrāhīm ibn al-Mahdī, in turn relates the anecdote to the *tunbūr*-player and historian Jaḥẓa, who tells it to his friend al-Iṣbahānī. Jaḥẓa and al-Iṣbahānī are both reliable historians. Their versions, as this story illustrates, include the participating musicians who were present during the event concerning their master, and then told the story to his son, all of this in the context of the princely household.

The anecdote emphasizes the theme of the ownership of songs and the rights of composers. To protect his rights, the composer resorts to musical changes in his performance in order to prevent other singers from acquiring his song. Only after receiving a handsome remuneration does the composer consent to transmit his song without alteration, and then only to the musician who paid for it. The scale of reward is hierarchical; in this case, the reward of the caliph is double that of the prince. The lewd proverb, introduced here as a metaphor, adds an element of humor to the story, as does the composer's insistence that he be paid the proper amount by the receiver of the song.

I was informed by Jaḥẓa[43] who said: I was informed by Hibat-Allāh ibn Ibrāhīm ibn al-Mahdī[44] who said: I was informed by *both* Rayyiq and Shāriya who said:

> One day our master—they meant my father[45]—was at the *majlis* of [the caliph] Muḥammad al-Amīn [d.198/813], and the singers were present. Yaḥyà al-Makkī [*ca.*100/ 718–218/833][46] sang—and the melody is in the *light-heavy īqāʿ*[47]—:

ṣawt[48]

A bosom friend of mine whom   *Has neither requited nor
   I loved madly   thanked [me]
But my name to him is invoked   *When he becomes frightened
                                          or falls on his face[49]

So our master asked that it be repeated, [for he] wished to learn it, [but] Yaḥyà kept on distorting it.[50] Al-Amīn noticed this, and ordered [that he be rewarded] twenty thousand dirhams,[51] and ordered him to repeat the song and abstain from mixing it up *(takhlīt)*.[52] So [Yaḥyà] invoked God in his favor, kissed the floor before him, and repeated the song, and sang it well and bettered it (جوّده). Then [Ibrāhīm] asked him to repeat it, but Yaḥyà said to him: "I won't be happy about giving it to you unless recompensed from your own money, and I won't assist you [in learning] it, because this money I have [just] received is my master's. Therefore, why should *you* take *my*[53] song!" Al-Amīn laughed, and ordered Ibrāhīm [to give Yaḥyà] ten thousand dirhams and Ibrāhīm [ordered that it be] brought.[54] Yaḥyà kissed his hand,[55] and repeated the song, and sang it well and bettered it. He saw Mukhāriq [d. *ca*.232/847] and 'Allūyah [d.236/850] raising their eyes, looking [opportunely and eagerly] (يتطلّعان) to learn the song, [and] so he abruptly cut off the song, turned towards them, and said: "A portion of the testicle of the elderly master is enough to cover the anuses of a number of boys.[56] By God, I shall not repeat it in your presence." Then he turned to our master—they meant Ibrāhīm ibn al-Mahdī—and said: "O master, I shall come to you[r palace], so that you learn it from me well and no one would share it with you." So he came and repeated it until [Ibrāhīm] learned it, and we learned with him.[57]

Although not comprehensive, the material presented here provides a very good idea of the sort of problems one is likely to encounter in medieval Arabic sources dealing with music. Many intertwined contextual decisions are needed in order to translate the sources and make them accessible to the modern reader.

NOTES

I am grateful to the Social Sciences and Humanities Research Council of Canada and the University of Toronto for supporting my research from 1987–92 on Arabic and Persian music sources. My thanks to Professors Richard Blackburn, Chair of the Department of Middle East and Islamic Studies and Carl Morey, Dean of the Faculty of Music, University of Toronto, for nominating my project and to Professors Mantle

Hood, University of Maryland, Michael Marmura and Andrew Hughes, University of Toronto, and Ali Jihad Racy, University of California, for their letters of support. I also thank Professor Claude V. Palisca for his helpful remarks about editing and translating texts during the conference.

1. For further details, see H. G. Farmer *The Sources of Arabian Music* 2d ed (Leiden 1965); A. Shiloah *The Theory of Music in Arabic writings (c.900–1900): Descriptive Catalogue of Manuscripts in Libraries of Europe and the U.S.A. RISM* BX (Munich 1979).

2. On the fine arts, including paintings in books and palaces, carvings, and inlaying of *objets d'art*, see Farmer *Islam: Musikgeschichte in Bildern Musik des Mittelalters und der Renaissance* 3 edd. H. Besseler and M. Schneider (Leipzig 1966).

3. My father and his two brothers were Levantine Christians who worked as professional translators (Arabic into French and English and vice versa). It is noteworthy that Levantine Nestorian Christians in the ninth century translated Greek treatises into Arabic (often *via* Syriac), and that Levantine Christians in the nineteenth and twentieth centuries translated literary and scientific works from French and English into Arabic.

4. This is not to imply that English is poor and Arabic rich. I refer here to a problem found in any translation when one must supply more than one English word to give the meaning of one Arabic word. The reverse is also true, for one often must use several Arabic words to give the precise meaning of one English word.

5. The root of the Arabic verb is trilateral (less often quadrilateral). It is known among Arabists as form one of the verb. Out of this root it is possible to derive nine forms (e.g., causative, reflexive, etc.), the total number of verb forms including the root being ten. (A few verbs may have more than ten forms.) They may be used in the active or passive voice, and out of both one can fashion verbal nouns, adjectives, and adverbs. Arabic dictionaries (Arabic to Arabic or Arabic to English) list all ten forms, derivative nouns, adjectives, and adverbs under the root. Thus, the translations or *les mots justes* sought by the translator can be found under more than one verb form and more than one of the derived verbal nouns, adjectives, or adverbs. As my colleague Professor Todd Lawson of McGill University so eloquently put it, we have here a "symphony of meanings" which translators ignore at their peril.

6. For instance, the Arabic word *īqā'* means rhythm, rhythmic mode, meter, and tempo; it also implies the concept of dynamics and timbre. Such a word is best left transliterated, with its many meanings entered in the glossary.

7. There are many cases, however, in which both English transliteration and Arabic script should be used; for instance, the words *qiṭ'a* (قطعة) and *qaṭ'aa* (قطعم) in Example 9.

8. I am presently working on a third draft of an English translation of this manuscript as part of a forthcoming book, *Rhythmic Theories in Arabic Writings from 750–970 A.D.* For other studies of the manuscript, see George Dimitri Sawa, *Music Performance Practice in the Early 'Abbāsid Era, 132 A.H./750 A.D.-320 A.H./932 A.D.* (Toronto 1989), "Al-Fārābī Theory of the *Iqā'*: An Empirically Derived Medieval Model of Rhythmic Analysis" *Progress Reports in Ethnomusicology* 1 (1983–4) 1–32.

9. I have consistently left the word *īqā'* and its plural form *īqā'āt* in a transliterated form, except for the title of the treatise. There I have translated *īqā'āt* as "rhythms," so that the subject of the book can be identified easily by the reader.

10. *Nuḥṣī* is the first-person plural of *aḥṣà*, which is the fourth form of the verb *ḥaṣà*. (a) *Aḥṣà* means to number, count, calculate, reckon, compute, reach the last number of, collect into an aggregate by number, enumerate. See E. W. Lane *An Arabic-English Lexicon* (London 1863; Beirut 1968) 2:587; H. Wehr *A Dictionary of Modern Written Arabic* ed. J. M. Cowan (Wiesbaden 1974; Beirut 1980) 183. (b) To retain in one's memory, understand, know altogether (as it is said of God: He comprehends everything by His knowledge; nothing escapes Him thereof, small or great), to attain a comprehensive and complete knowledge of a subject.

In this case, I have chosen to translate *aḥṣà* by three verbs/phrases that are semantically related: "enumerate," "classify," and "attain a basic comprehension of." Al-Fārābī does indeed *classify* the *īqā'āt* into three categories—*light, light-heavy,* and *heavy*—with further subdivisions; by *classifying* them, he *enumerates* them, leaving nothing out (in his mind at least), even *īqā'āt* used in speech and poetry, an approach he seems not to have used in the *Grand Book of Music.* Besides *classifying* and *enumerating* them, al-Fārābī devises a system *to attain a basic comprehension of* the theory of rhythms, one which enables the reader to delve further into rhythmic analysis and compound rhythms, thereby "understanding," "knowing altogether," and "comprehending everything by one's knowledge," as in meaning (b). And this meaning in turn reverts back to "reaching the last number of a thing," "enumerating," and "classifying," as in meaning (a).

11. In the sense of understanding the essence of their *fundamental* form as well as the idiosyncratic variation techniques that suit them individually.

12. *Nakhtari'uhā* means to originate, invent, devise, innovate, make, do, produce, cause something to be or exist for the first time. I have chosen "to cause them to exist for the first time," because it seems to me to be the most accurate translation of the intended meaning. However, it is possible to argue against my interpretation on the grounds that this notational system goes back to Al-Fārābī *Grand Book of Music*. What we see here is not an innovation, but rather a renovation of two of his previous systems of notation: one in the *Grand Book of Music*, which was improved once in *Kitāb al-Īqā'āt (Book of Rhythms)* Istanbul: Topkapi Sarayi, MS. III, Ahmet 1878 ff.160b-67a, and again in *Kitāb Ihsā' al-Īqā'āt*. The notation system involves alphabetic symbols, phonetics, arithmetic and geometric signs, as well as explanatory captions under the various parts of a notated *īqā'*. I have used the general word "notation" to translate *rasm*, although this word also means writing, mark, sign, trace, vestige, relic, remain, drawing, sketch, description, and prescription. See Lane *Arabic-English Lexicon* 3:1084–5. The implied meanings of "writing," "mark," "sign," "drawing," "sketch," "description," and "prescription" are evident in Al-Fārābī's notational system. See, for instance, Figure 1, the first notated example on f.64a, which indeed looks like a drawing with writings, signs, and descriptions.

Regarding "description" and "prescription," the reader should realize that these words do not carry the same meaning as the ones in Charles Seeger's well-known article, "Prescriptive and Descriptive Music Writing" *Musical Quarterly* 44 (1958) 184–95. Though Al-Fārābī's rhythmic notation in this treatise is intended for analysis and indicates tempo, dynamics, and timbre, it is pitchless, and thus it can be construed neither as descriptive nor as prescriptive. Al-Fārābī's notation system, then, is limited to a didactic purpose: the teaching of rhythmic analysis. Since the notation system is incomplete, the word chosen by al-Fārābī, *rasm*, probably points to such nuances as "trace," "vestige," "relic," and "remain." It should also be noted that the word *rasm* is used by some Islamic philosophers to refer to description (*imperfect* definition) as opposed to *ḥadd* (*perfect* definition). See B. Carra de Vaux "*Ḥadd*" *Encyclopaedia of Islam* edd. C. Pellat *et al* (Leiden 1971) 3:20–1.

13. Namely, the *Grand Book of Music*, as al-Fārābī himself states on f.60. See Example 3. It is curious that he does not mention the less polished *Book of Rhythms*, which he must have composed before the present work.

14. These arts are music, poetry, speech, and dance. The new approach in this treatise comprises the many music examples, taken from practical music and used to explain the theory of *īqāʿ*, and the assumption that the reader will make further theoretical investigations in the *Grand Book of Music*.

15. (عِبَارَة) means word, writing, expression, phrase, explanation, or interpretation. See Lane *Arabic-English Lexicon* 5:1938.

16. For example, the *īqāʿāt* known as *al-hazaj* and *al-ramal* retain their names. Those al-Fārābī found in practice, but without names, (or rather with names that had fallen into desuetude) are to be named according to what they resemble; e.g., the 7/8 classified as the *fifth-light (al-khafīf al-khāmis)*, because of its similarity to *al-hazaj*, will be called *al-muḍāriʿ li-al-hazaj*, which means "the one similar to *al-hazaj*." Likewise, the *sixth-light (al-khafīf al-sādis)*, because of the abundance of attacks in a cycle, will be called *al-khafīf al-wāfir*, meaning "the abundant *light*."

17. In the published version of the translation, the entire Arabic text will be reproduced in facsimile.

18. *Heavy*, a literal translation of the Arabic *thaqīl*, denotes the rhythmic modes belonging to the slow species.

19. Known also as simply *ramal*.

20. This passage appears in the following sources: Istanbul: Köprülüzāde MS 953 [Köprülü] f.365; Leiden: Universiteitsbibliotheek MS Or. 651 f.102a; Milan: Biblioteca Ambrosiana MS 289 ff.158a-b; Istanbul: Ragıp Paşa MS 876 ff.149b-50a; Princeton: University Library Ms Garrett 1984 f.75b; *Kitab al-Mūsīqī al-Kabīr* [Cairo] ed. Ghaṭṭās ʿAbd-al-Malik Khashaba; rev. Maḥmūd Aḥmad al-Ḥifnī (Cairo 1967) 986; *Grand traité de musique* [Paris] trans. R. d'Erlanger (Paris 1930 and 1935) 2:27.

21. As, for example, the nominative, accusative, or genitive case-endings for indefinite nouns—*un, an, in*—as in *walad-un, walad-an*,

or *walad-in* ("a boy" in the nominative, accusative, and genitive cases respectively).

22. As, for example, the nominative, accusative, or genitive case-endings for definite nouns—*u, a, i*—as in *walad-u, walad-a,* or *walad-i* ("the boy" in the nominative, accusative, and genitive cases respectively).

23. In brief, *rawm* is an obscure and slurred vowel sound, and *ishmām*, less obvious than *rawm*, is extremely feeble. See Lane *Arabic-English Lexicon* 3:1193. According to grammarians, a *rawm* occurs when a final vowel is obscurely sounded, or when a slurred *ayyu, ayyi* is shortened to *ay* ("which/what"): e.g., *ayyuhumā* becomes *ay-humā* ("which of the two"); *ayyumā* becomes *ayma* (as in *ayma taqūlu* or "what do you say?"); *ayyū shay'in* becomes *aysh* ("what"). See W. Wright *A Grammar of the Arabic Language* (Cambridge 1874; Beirut 1974) 1:276. An *ishmām*, on the other hand, occurs when a vowel is given the "scent" or "flavor" of another. For instance, when *u* is given a flavor or scent of *i*, producing *ü*: e.g., when *rudda* becomes *rüdda* and *shudda* becomes *shüdda*; or when *i* is given the flavor or scent of *u* (known as *ishmām al-ḍamm* or *ḥaraka bayna al-ḍamm wa al-kasr*)—as do some readers of the *Qur'ān do*—producing *ü*: e.g., when *qīla* becomes *qüla*. See Wright *Grammar* 1:71, 84. See also Abū Abd-Allāh Muḥammad ibn Aḥmad ibn Yūsuf al-Kātib al-Khuwārizmī (d.387/997) *Kitāb Mafātīḥ al-'Ulūm* ed. G. van Vloten (Leiden 1895) 44.

24. In d'Erlanger *Grand traité de musique*, one reads *matha*. In the Leiden copy, this word is illegible. Al-Kātib has *masha*. See Al-Ḥasan ibn Aḥmad ibn 'Alī al-Kātib (fifth-eleventh century) *Kitāb Kamāl Adab al-Ghinā'* ed. Khashaba; rev. al-Hifni (Cairo 1975) 85–6, 94; trans. A. Shiloah *La perfection des connaissances musicales. Kitāb Kamāl Adab al-Ġinā'* (Paris 1972) 132–3, 142. The word *masha* means a rubbing, tinge, shade, trace, or touch of something. See Wehr *Dictionary* 907. It also means a sign, mark, or trait of beauty, for example. See Lane *Arabic-English Lexicon* 7:2714. The meanings of the root-word *masha*, as well as those derived from the root, give us important semantic tools for understanding more fully the nature of *masha*.

The following discussion summarizes the meaning of related words. See Lane *Arabic-English Lexicon* 7:2714–5. (a) *Masha* derives from the verb *masaha*, which means to wipe, pass the hand over something, compass, anoint—hence the possible derivation of *masīḥ* ("the Messiah, the Christ, the Anointed") from *masaḥa* ("to anoint")—stroke (as in stroking one's beard), rub, strike gently. (b) *Masaḥ-un*, also from the verb *masaḥa*, means paucity of flesh on the posterior and thighs, smallness of the buttocks and their sticking together, paucity of flesh on the thighs. (c) *Mashā'* refers to a woman having little flesh on the posterior and thighs, and/or no bulk to her chest. (In the colloquial Arabic of Egypt, the word *mash* refers to the flat chest or buttocks of the female). (d) *Masīḥ* refers to a silver coin whose impression has been obliterated, or to smooth and soft feet that have no fissures or cracks so that they repel water when it falls on them. (e) *Amsaḥu mashā'* means a flat piece of bare land with small pebbles and without plants or herbage; *amsaḥu* also means a flat foot. (f) *Amsaḥa* refers to a man whose inner thighs rub together so that they become sore and chapped, or whose inner knee is inflamed by the roughness of his garment. (g) *Mamsūḥ* denotes something that is altered from its proper form or make, and by extension, a eunuch whose testicles have been extirpated. *'Aḍudun mamsūḥatun* means an arm having little flesh from shoulder to elbow. And *mamsūḥu al-alyatayni* means small buttocks that cleave to the bone.

The nature of the *masha* alludes to a change in make-up, a missing element, and incompleteness and lack of fullness. The action required to produce it, in a literal sense, is a gentle strike, and in a figurative sense, a rubbing or wiping (a) and (f). The sound is neither resounding or loud, but rather dull, flat, barren, sterile, non-vibrant (b), (c), (d), (e), and (g). The level of the sound is nothing more than a tinge, a shade, a touch, a trace, a sound with little bulk or substance (b), (c), (d), and (g).

25. The phonemes here are the sounds of the *nunnation*, short vowel, slurred and obscure vowel, and less than slurred and obscure vowel.

26. This directive contradicts the information given previously. Neither d'Erlanger nor Khashaba (the Cairene editor) comment on this problem: in the Cairo edition, *moderate* equals short vowel and *soft* equals *rawm* or *ishmām* on page 986, whereas on page 987 *moderate* equals *ishmām* and *soft* equals *rawm*. Moreover, the information on page 987 of the Cairo edition is incorrect: though al-Fārābī intended to follow a grammatical model, he (or perhaps a copyist) confuses

the hierarchical classification of _ishmām_ and _rawm_ by considering the _ishmām_ as a _moderate_ attack, thus placing it ahead of the _soft ishmām_.

27. This passage is taken from the following sources: Köprülü ff.374–5, Leiden f.104b, Milan f.161b, Ragıp f.153b, Princeton f.77b, Cairo 1011, Paris 2:35.

28. This passage is found in the following sources: Köprülü f.378, Leiden f.105a, Milan f.163a, Ragıp f.154b, Princeton f.78b, Cairo 1019, Paris 2:38.

29. This passage comes from the following sources: Köprülü f.379, Leiden f.105a, Milan f.163a, Ragıp f.155a, Princeton f.78b, Cairo 1020, Paris 2:39.

30. The _gradation_ is a rhythmic ornamental technique that fills a measure (or measures) with notes of equal duration.

31. This passage is taken from the following sources: Köprülü f.380, Leiden f.105b, Milan f.163b, Ragıp f.155a, Princeton f.79a, Cairo 1021, Paris 2:39.

32. In Köprülü, Leiden, Cairo, "brilliancy" (البهاء); in Milan, Princeton, Ragıp, "purity" (النقاء). The latter must be a copyist's error. A few lines later it becomes clear that the word _bahā'_ was definitely meant, because it appears in a different form, the comparative adjective _abhà_.

33. The era, not mentioned explicitly here, is that of Hārūn al-Rashīd. See a similar anecdote in the _Book of Songs_, (Cairo 1923–74) 5:272, that identifies the period. For the significance of the monthly stipend, see M. M. Ahsan, _Social Life Under the Abbasids: 170–289 A.H./786–902 A.D._ (London 1979) 148; Sawa _Music Performance Practice_ 6.

34. This is most likely Muḥammad ibn Maḥmūd ibn Manṣūr ibn Rashīd al-Khuzā'ī, also known as Abū Bakr ibn abī al-Azhar (d.325/937). He was a writer, grammarian, and story-teller from Baghdād. The title of some of his works indicate that his writing is historical, anecdotal, and entertaining in nature: _The Jumble Concerning Anecdotes About the Caliphs al-Musta'īn and al-Mu'tazz; The History; Stories About the Wise Men From Among the Crazy._ See 'Umar Riḍā Kaḥḥāla _Mu'jam al-Mu'allifīn. Tarājim Muṣannifī al-Kutub al-'Arabiyya_ 15 vols. (Damascus 1957–61) 2:14.

35. He is an extremely important narrator of poetic and musical anecdotes in the *Book of Songs*. His narratives come from "genetic" first-hand sources: his father Isḥāq al-Mawṣilī (d.235/850) and his grandfather Ibrāhīm al-Mawṣilī (d.188/804).

36. Al-Iṣbahānī informs us that she died in the city of al-Baṣra, but gives no dates for her birth or death. The daughter of Shuhda, a mourner from the holy city of Makka, she was a famous singer, lutenist, composer, and educator. She taught her slave-boy, Mukhāriq (d.227/842), the art of singing and playing the *'ūd*. Mukhāriq later became a leading singer and composer in the courts of the early 'Abbāsid era. See *Book of Songs* 6:260–2.

37. Literally, "the best beater or striker on the lute."

38. The Arabic text does not say *tu'allimunī* ("taught me") but rather *tuḍāribunī*, a much more precise term. Not only does it mean to teach, but it also explains the method of teaching. *Tuḍāribunī* is the third form (conjugated in the third-person feminine imperfect tense) of the verb *ḍaraba*, and this form implies the notion of reciprocity and conation. See G. M. Wickens *Arabic Grammar: A First Workbook* (Cambridge 1980) 66. Thus, the instrumental lessons consisted of the master, 'Ātika, playing first alone, and Isḥāq then repeating what she played (reciprocity of striking the strings of the *'ūd*); also 'Ātika playing, and Isḥāq trying to copy her (conation).

39. The word *ḍarb* is an obscure and complicated technical term with many meanings: (a) striking, as in striking a percussion instrument or a string; (b) a rhythmic mode in the thirteenth century, as in *ḍarb al-ramal* (for *īqā' al-ramal*); see Farmer *A History of Arabian Music to the XIIIth Century* (London 1929; 1973) 203; O. Wright *The Modal System of Arab and Persian Music: AD 1250–1300* (London 1978) 217–20; (c) the last foot of a hemistich (a meaning unrelated to this story); (d) kind, species, sort, and so on, in a general sense; (e) instrumental style or technique, as in the *Book of Songs* 5:272. From the context of the story it seems that (b) and (c) are unlikely meanings. The vague meanings of (a) and (d) could lead to the conjecture that *ḍarb* means an instrumental piece, an instrumental exercise, a playing technique, style, or ornament, or an instrumental rendition of a song. A parallel anecdote in the *Book of Songs* has Zalzal as the *'ūd* teacher and 'Ātika as the voice teacher, and instead of *ḍarb* we find the word *ṭarq*, which also means "striking." So it may be that 'Ātika taught him both singing and lute playing.

40. That is to say, the thirty thousand dirhams were paid partly in cash money and partly in kind.

41. The proverb may or may not be included in the major collections of Arabic medieval proverbs. I was not able to spend time looking for it in these sources, which do not have indices and therefore must be perused in their entirety. This is disappointing because the sayings are usually accompanied by short commentaries.

42. Both were later freed, and became famous singers.

43. A descendant of the Barmakid family of viziers, he was a close friend of al-Iṣbahānī, a writer, a ṭunbūr-player, and a narrator of musical events. One of his famous books often used in the *Book of Songs* is *The Book of Ṭunbūr-Players*. See K̲h̲ayr al-Dīn al-Ziriklī *Al-A'lām* 8 vols. 4th ed (Beirut 1979) 1:107.

44. A prince and the son of Prince Ibrāhīm ibn al-Mahdī, he was a poet, a fine connoisseur of music, and a narrator who witnessed first hand the musical performances of his father and his father's colleagues. He died in 275/888.

45. The singer-prince Ibrāhīm ibn al-Mahdī.

46. See E. Neubauer "Musiker am Hof der frühen 'Abbāsiden" (Ph.D. diss. Frankfurt am Main 1965) 207.

47. This could be a short form for the *first-light-heavy* (an īqā' in 4/4), or the *second-light-heavy* (an īqā' in 5/4). It could also refer to an īqā' overlooked by al-Fārābī.

48. A technical term used to denote a poem that has been set to music.

49. Even worse than not being reciprocated, the name of the beloved—instead of being evoked as a blessing (as is normally the custom)—is here invoked as if it were a bad spirit to be repulsed.

50. The Arabic verb *afsada* (fourth form of *fasada*) means to spoil or distort. Thus the connotation here is that the musical change or distortion is not a positive one.

51. Farmer, who says ten thousand, has confused the amount given by the caliph with that given by the prince. See *History of Arabian Music* 113–4.

52. The Arabic verbal noun *tak̲h̲līṭ* means confusing, mixing-up, disordering, and thus, as in *afsada* above, it carries negative connotations for this kind of musical change.

53. Underlining by the author.

54. Since Ibrāhīm was not at home, but rather in the caliph's palace, he has to order a servant to bring the money.

55. The hand of the caliph, though it is possible that "his" refers to the hand of Ibrāhīm.

56. Obviously, Yahyà does not want to transmit his composition to Mukhāriq and 'Allūyah, for they have paid nothing. Since they were more than eager to learn it, he gets angry and addresses them in a condescending manner: the obscenity of the metaphor aside, he belittles them by implying that the portion of the song, heard by these two younger singers is all they can digest. The song, after all, is composed by a venerable master, and it is therefore difficult to learn. And these younger musicians have not accumulated the wisdom and experience needed to learn the entire song. The ensuing discussion gives more details concerning the metaphor.

"The portion of the testicle of the elderly master": the elderly master refers to Yahyà himself, the testicle refers to the song, and its portion to precisely the segment of the song Yahyà had sung before cutting off his performance. (The Arabic text has "portion (*qit'a* قطعة) of the testicle," and about the sudden interruption it has "he abruptly cut off (*qata'a* قطع) the song." The implication, however, is that only a "portion" was sung; moreover, the morphology of *qit'a* and *qata'a* adds to this reading, since the verb *qata'a* ("to cut off") is the root from which *qit'a* ("portion") is derived. This derivation is very clear in the Arabic script.

"Boys" refers to 'Allūyah and Mukhāriq. They are quite young compared to Yahyà, who is said to have lived for 120 years. See Neubauer *Musiker am Hof* 207; *Book of Songs* 6:174. If the event occurred when al-Amīn was assuming the caliphate (809–813), and if the longevity of Yahyà is accurate, then Yahyà must have been in his nineties at the time.

"Is enough to cover the anuses of a number of boys" refers to the size of the orifices, which must be narrow. Since only a "portion" of a testicle is needed to cover many of them. The size alludes to the limited musical abilities of the younger singers. On the narrowness of the anus as an indication of limited ability, see Lane *Arabic-English Lexicon* 4:1305.

57. Yahyà allows the slave-girls to learn the song because they are the property of Ibrāhīm, who has already paid his fee.

Preparing Editions and Translations of Humanist Treatises on Music: Franchino Gaffurio's *Theorica Musice* (1492)

Walter Kurt Kreyszig

University of Saskatchewan
and
University of Vienna

Humanist texts on music theory, because of their intrinsic nature, present an array of problems. This is partly the result of the wide selection of sources, ranging from classical texts, poetry and prose included, to the writings of the Church Fathers, as well as more contemporary writings. Beyond this, the Latin language, like other Romance languages, has undergone a number of significant changes, all of which amount to a freer use of both syntax and grammar.

The translation of music-theoretical treatises has benefitted from several excellent models found in two series, namely, *Music Theory Translation Series*[1] and *Greek and Latin Music Theory*.[2] Further, Mathiesen's *A Style Guide for Text Criticism, Translation, and the Preparation of Camera-Ready Typescript*[3] offers a set of useful guidelines for translation.

In the preparation of critical editions, we have even fewer models to emulate. Here, the series *Greek and Latin Music Theory* as well as Mathiesen's already mentioned guidelines offer some insight. In this endeavor, however, we are principally indebted to classical scholarship, in particular the pathbreaking editions of Boethius' works, prepared by Gottfried Friedlein.[4]

Associated with the editing and translating of Latin humanist texts are numerous problems. Some of these stem from the complexity of the material presented, whereas others relate directly to the fusion of the many linguistic traditions in the sources consulted. Franchino Gaffurio's *Theorica musice* exemplifies these linguistic traditions, and thus offers a particular challenge for the preparation of a critical edition and translation. Using specific passages, the present study develops a set of guidelines derived from the actual completion of an edition and translation of this treatise.[5]

The study will show the extent to which classical scholarship has had a vital impact on the editing of humanist texts. Indeed, the inevitable reliance on the work of classicists will undoubtedly continue to inform our endeavor. In this way, we are able to assure an edition that not only reflects the original intention of the author, but also forms the basis for a reliable translation.

Our examination concentrates on three principal areas, that is, the preparation of the edition in view of Gaffurio's language, the printer's layout of the page, and the orthography; the sources and their identification by Gaffurio; the preparation of the translation, foremost the vexing problem of terminology. The concluding section presents the implementation, in a short continuous passage from the *Theorica musice,* of some of these issues and guidelines.

THE PREPARATION OF THE EDITION. If classical scholars are the beneficiaries of a well-established tradition of reliable critical editions[6] of primary documents from various periods, complemented by general studies on the procedures of editing,[7] historians and theorists of music have only more recently followed the footsteps of the classicists in giving greater consideration to the preparation of critical editions of treatises. Indeed, a renewed interest in such endeavors in the discipline of music is manifested not only by such long-standing projects as *The-saurus Linguae Latinae, Thesaurus Linguae Graecae,* and *Lexicon Musicum Latinum,*[8] but also by recent advances in computer technology, as in the latest undertaking, *Thesaurus Musicarum Latinarum,* a new full-text database aimed at a comprehensive indexing of Latin music theory from the Middle Ages and early Renaissance, preserved in both manuscripts and printed sources.[9]

The foundation for critical editions of documents relevant to musical scholarship was laid by classicists during the last century. For example, Friedlein's editions of Boethius' two major treatises, *De institutione arithmetica* and *De institutione musica* (published in 1867) are still highly regarded for their careful preparation of the text and meticulous collation of the many manuscript sources. The latter has served as a basis for the recent translation by Calvin M. Bower.[10] Friedlein's work as well as more recent editions, notably those of Andres Briner,[11] Renate Federhofer-Königs,[12] Jan Herlinger,[13] Hans Schmid,[14] and Albert Seay[15] have provided guidance for preparing a critical edition of Gaffurio's *Theorica musice.*

Gaffurio's treatise, steeped in the tradition of humanism, demonstrates the revival of ancient learning most obviously in the multiplicity of disciplines mentioned and breadth of topics discussed as well as in the diversity of sources cited. The treatise exists in two versions: the 1492 publication in Milan,[16] and an earlier Naples version of 1480, the first printed source in music, with the title *Theoricum opus musice discipline.*[17] Whereas the *Theoricum opus* as well as Gaffurio's other two major works, *Practica musicae* (Milan 1496)[18] and *De harmonia musicorum instrumentorum opus* (Milan 1518),[19] exist not only in printed form but also, at least in part, in manuscripts,[20] the *Theorica musice* survives in a number of copies of the original publication, copies scattered across Europe and North America.[21] The status of the sources, as deplorable as the absence of manuscripts for the *Theorica musice* may seem, especially since the origin of many errors in the treatise cannot be determined with any certainty, adds a new question to the present examination: how to formulate editorial procedures based exclusively on material transmitted in printed form? The focus here on various aspects of the Latin language, including orthography, syntax, and so on, extends the results of an earlier examination of editorial procedures for Latin texts preserved in manuscripts, the topic of the Twenty-Third Conference on Editorial Problems.[22] The deliberations of classical scholars are usually restricted to considering the manuscript tradition, a mode of transmission that poses many problems. This fact influences the availability of published guidelines for printed sources; for example, the Leiden system concentrates solely on manuscripts.[23] Yet, as the modern edition of the *Theorica musice* shows, even the printed version of a document does not necessarily provide an accurate reflection of the author's intention, and this factor leads to emendations and thus to deliberate decisions on editorial procedures.

My critical edition of Gaffurio's *Theorica musice* is based on the original printed version of 1492 in the copy located in the *Beinecke Rare Book and Manuscript Library* at Yale University, as well as on published facsimile editions.[24] The earlier versions of the *Theorica musice* and the *Theoricum opus musice discipline* have also been taken into account.[25] To summarize, variants in the respective publications concern orthography and syntax as well as substantive changes in content from the 1480 to the 1492 versions.[26] These matters lie beyond the scope of this essay.

No uniform guidelines for editing humanist documents have been developed.[27] This lacuna may be the result of the recency of such undertakings and of the diversity of the primary material. As a consequence, the widely accepted guidelines for classical texts put forth by Martin West[28] provide very general editorial methods, and these are used in my work. Beyond this, editors of a humanist text must generate their own procedures based on careful scrutiny of the text. This is why I shall give a somewhat detailed outline of the procedures used in the critical edition of Gaffurio's *Theorica musice*.

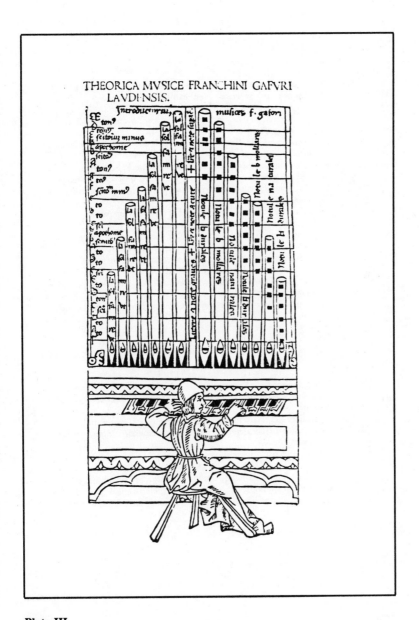

Plate III
Franchino Gaffurio *Theorica musice* (Milan 1492)
title page.

Errores Impreſſoris negligentia commiſſi in hoc opere :quibus & ſententia ua-
riari & mens lectoris dubia reddi poteſt corrigantur hoc modo.

IN PRIMO LIBRO.

In Primo Capitulo i linea q̄ icipit natura eblectamētuᴙ corrige oblectamētoᴙ
Item in linea quæ Incipit chil ram faclie Corrige facile
Item in linea quæ incipit Principes ac rerum publicaᴙ ſenat° rubia corrige tuba.
Item in linea quæ Incipit percepi poſſe Corrige percipi
Item i calce primi capituli i linea quæ icipit eis ſolertioreſ.pſecto corrige ꝓ fecto
In Secundo Capitulo in linea quæ Incipit uis ſtellā ſemitonio Corrige ſemitoniū
In tertio Capitulo in ſeptima linea que incipit partes coniungat aconiuncta cor-
ge coniuncta.
Item in linea quæ Incipit ut Cenſorinus refert partes Corrige partus
Item in linea quæ incipit impare corrige impares
In Q̄ uinto Capitulo in linea quæ Incipit qppe quæ in aio cōſta Corrige conſtat.
Item in linea que incipit ſici conſtitutione perfecto corrige profecto.
In Sexto Capitulo in linea quæ Incipit pondere non pſſit Corrige poſſit :

IN SECVNDO LIBRO.

In calce Q̄ uinti capituli in linea que incipit conſonantiam implet ſuperbipartienti corrige duplæſuperbipartienti.
Iré in ꝓxima ibi linea quæ Incipit ſuperbipartienti Corrige duplæſupbipartiēti·

IN TERTIO LIBRO

In Secundo Capitulo in linea que incipit preciſe: eſt quæ corrige cꝗ
In Q̄ uarto Capitulo in linea quæ Incipit Q̄ ui ſi eo Corrige ꝗ ſi eo.
In Q̄ uinto Capitulo in linea que incipit Reſtat inſuper ſcitu dignum quandā
natuiæ ſecretam adde diſpoſitione.

IN Q̄ VARTO LIBRO.

In Secūdo Capitulo in linea auodecima q̄ icipit 9 ad 4 ſeſqualterā corrige ₆ ad 4
In Capitulo tertio in linea q̄ icipit mox fiēt.≈ 18 7 itē ≈ 5°.numer°corrige itē ≈ 5 ₆
numerus
Item in linea quæ Incipit ſonantia in minoribus Corrige i maioribus.
In Capitulo ſexto i linea ſeptia quæ icipit tinua detraxerimus deleatur geminata
quia uacat
Itē i linea ſequēti q̄ Incipit to ablatæ ꝓportionis .ſ. ſeſꝗoctauæ Corrige ſeſꝗtiæ

IN LIBRO Q̄ VINTO ET VLTIMO.

In Capitulo ſecundo in linea quæ incipit nio & tono q̄ corrige quam
In Capitulo ſexto i prima linea q̄ icipit Latinoᴙ puidētia imitaa corrige imitata
Itē i linea q̄ icipit.int̄ hāc & ſecūdā precedēte Corrige int̄ hāc ſedā & precedēte

ad numerum.⹂43.intercidit:primam semitonii minoris formam exprimit ex ipsis primis minimis numeris exquisitam atque deductâ. At quoniam prædictum est hoc minus semitonium rectum toni dimidium non implere : id cuidenniori demonstratione probandum fore duxi. Nam cum numerorum.⹂43.et.⹂56. differentia : tredecim tantum unitatibus sit:si ipsam deciesocties multiplicemus differentiam non reddet totum minorem sed deficiet a tota ipsius minoris summa:nam fient.⹂34. qui minor est quam.⹂43. ·Verû quom deciesnouies multiplicata fuerit ipsa differentia scilicet.13.ipsum minorem scilicet.⹂43.huiusmodi multiplicatio superuadet:fient nançः.⹂47.Continet itaçः ipsa differentia minus q̄ decimamoctauam ipsius minoris partem:plus uero q̄ decimamnonam. Ex quo opus est semironium omne :ad hoc ut integro toni dimidio conseruetur :inter sesquisextam decimam & sesquidecimamseptimam collocari : quod quidem impossibile est:nam ut superius monstratum est:Proportio sesquioctaua in duas inæquas partes diuiditur:ut quæ euenit inter.i8.et.i₆.quoniam naturaliter numerus.i7.intercidit:non eandem proportionem retinent .i7.ad.i₆.quâ prebant. 18.ad.17.igitur ipsa sesquioctaua in duo æqua diuidi non posse monstratur Q d si fieri temptaretur:necesse esset aliquantulam de sesquisextadecima proportione auferre portionem sesquidecimæseptimæ applicandam quo æqualiter se haberent.quod quidem fieri nullatenns potest:quoniam sesquisextadecima nullam in se minorem habet particulam q̄ sesquisextamdecimam. s. indiuisibilē unitatem :quam integre inuiolabiliterçः nititur conseruare.Constat itaçः lucidius tonum in duo æqua diuidi non posse·Minus autem semitonium non attingit medietatem toni:quo fit ut si duplicatum fuerit:tonum perficere non possit :Igitur duo minora semitonia penum toni interuallum implere nó possunt. Id enim naturaliter euenit ut quem quicquid dimidium duplicatur:totum integrum ducit id cuius ante duplicationem dimidium erat:si autem ipsa duplicatio non perfecerit illud integrum sequitur ante duplicationem id quod duplicatum fuerat dimidium non fuisse. Verum si geminata particula superexcreuerit suum totum : tunc anteçः duplicaretur mai or erat parte dimidia .Illud igitur quod uere in cō fonanriis semitonium nuncupatur:minus est recto toni dimidio:quod uero relinquitur de toto tono maius est dimidia ipsius toni parte :quo fit ut semitoniũ maius dicatur . Q uanteçः semitonium minus recto toni dimidio minus est tanto Apothome integrum toni dimidium excedit. Et quoniam monstratum est semitonium inter.⹂56.et.⹂43. principaliter consistere:nunc in quibus minoribus numeris constet Apothome discutiēdum est.Si enim.⹂43.octauam possent recipere partem ita ut ad eum suus posset sesquioctauus comparari:tunc .⹂56.habitudo ad ipsius minoris sesquioctauum colata apothomen necessaria ratione probaret.sed quoniam ipse.⹂43. numerus octauam partem habere non potest

g i

finguli numeri octonario crefcant :& quidem . ≈ 4 3. numerus octies ductus numerum .i 9 4 4 .perficit:quibus dum propria fuperponatur octaua fcilicet .≈ 4 3.
mox hæ.≈ 1 8 7.Ité · ≈ 5 9 numer° crefcat octies numerū.≈ 0 4 8.códucetqui præ-
ductorū med uf collocet hoc mó

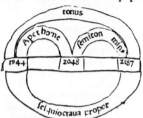

Tertius itaque terminus ad primum tonum ducit fefquioctaua
ratione compræhenfum.Secun-
dus uero ad primum apothomen
fed tertius ad fecund um femitonium minus idcirco quia in mino
ribus numeris maior euenit proportio & confequenter maior có
fonantia.in minoribus autem mi
nor. Atque in his primis apotho-
mes conftat proportio.cum femitonii minoris fpacium in.≈ 5 6 et .≈ 4 3. minimis
contineatur numeris.Sunt idcirco .i 9 4 4. et.≈ 0 4 8.in eadem proportione qua
≈ 4 3.&.≈ 5 6. quoniam . ≈ 4 3.&.≈ 5 6. funt octies multiplicati. Q uom enim
unus numerus duos quoflibet numeros multiplicauerit:tunc numeri qui ex ipfa
multiplicatione conducentur in eadem erunt proportione qua fuerunt hi numeri
quos multiplicator numerus multiplicauit . Monftrat tamen apertius toni diui-
fionem Phylolaus Pythagoricus ftatuens primum imparem numerum fcilicet
ternarium cum fuo quadrato qui nouenarius eft:hunc enim ternario multiplicat
& fiunt . ≈ 7 . qui ad . ≈4 . deducti tonum in fefquioctaua relatione cuftodiunt :
eorum quippe ternarius differentia eft : qui octies computatus numerum : ≈ 4 :
implet:nouies uero : ≈ 7 . perficit. Tonum quoq in femitoniū minus diuidit atq
Apothomen:horum differenciam coma effe dixit:afferens minus femitonium tredecim unitatibus conftare eo q inter . ≈ 5 .. & . ≈ 4 3 . præuifa fit differentia &
quia item is numerus . i 3 . ex nouenario & ternario atque unitate quæ in cunctis
numeris fingularem obtinet locum confiftit: ternariufq primus fit impar in nu -
mero naturali::atq nouenarius primus impar quadratus:idcirco cóftituto minor
femitonio in numero. i 3 . re'iquam . ≈ 7 . numeri partem quæ quattuordecim
unicatibus fupereft Apothomen cenfuit continere.At cum amborū fcilicet . i 3 .
& . i 4 . num rotum unitas differentiam teneat:unitatem ipfam loco comatis ar-
bitrat ur effe tenendam:totum q tonum . ≈ 7 . unitaribus fiftit:eo q inter . ≈ 4 3 .
et · ≈ 6 . numeros qui inter fe tono diftant:ipfe . ≈ 7 . numerus differentiam 'er-
uet. Ex iis uidetur inferri tonum conftare duobus femitoniis unoq comate:nam
ficut tonus Apothomen & minus femitonium compræhendit: femitonium uero
ab apothome differt comate : nihil aliud apothomen effe conftat q femitonium

The editing of humanist texts, unlike the editing of medieval or classical Latin texts,[29] is complicated from the outset by the quantity of primary sources from which the humanist author draws inspiration and information. Medieval authors generally base their knowledge on rather limited source material, especially in the fields of theology and law.[30] Humanist authors, however, in their persistent quest for new insights into ancient doctrine and practice through reviving pertinent documents, had a much wider array of sources at their disposal, sources unearthed by active manuscript and book hunting.[31]

The annotations to my edition of the *Theorica musice* address the thorny issue of textual emendations. Though existing editions of music-theoretical treatises do not exhibit a uniform format, they offer some procedural models. Careful study of these works reveals two distinct types of editions. The "diplomatic" type gives a literal reading of the original text with few, if any, emendations. A more recent type tries to give the reader a grammatically correct, rather than a literal, reading of the text. For Gaffurio's *Theorica musice* I have produced a corrected version in the main body of the text, with deviations from the 1492 print recorded in annotations, as well as incorporating some techniques associated with diplomatic editions. In general, my edition adheres to the standard North American editorial practice for critical texts (which includes corrections in the main body), and not to the European style (which relegates corrections to the annotations). Thus the edition and the translation are synchronized.

A few observations on Gaffurio's Latin are in order. The *Theorica musice*, written in humanist Latin, reveals a more complex syntax and an infinitely richer vocabulary than the medieval writings.[32] The elements that contribute to this syntactical complexity are: loose word order, grammatical freedom, a preponderance of infinitive verb forms as opposed to the conjugated verbs characteristic of medieval Latin, and frequent elliptical phraseology.[33] The expansion of Latin vocabulary, which began

in the Middle Ages, can be gaged by the introduction of pre-
fixes and suffixes to existing nouns and the formation of new
words, some of which are not to be found in standard classical
dictionaries.[34]

The diversity of source and literary traditions in the *Theorica
musice* is also manifested by Gaffurio's choice of words and syntax, even when he paraphrases or summarizes ideas from other
sources. Because of the heavy reliance on sources, a trademark
typical of humanist writing in general, Gaffurio traverses many
linguistic boundaries in the course of writing this treatise. In
the *Theorica musice* he uses classical authors, such as Horace
and Ovid, the patristic emulator of Biblical Latin, Saint Augustine, the scholastic writers, Boethius and Isidore of Seville,
who emulate classical Latin in their stylistic clarity, more recent
medieval writers, such as Giorgio Anselmi and Marchetto of
Padua, as well as practitioners of humanist Latin contemporary
to Gaffurio, such as Marsilio Ficino and Hermolao Barbaro.[35]

Orthographical changes must be carefully noted, for they have
a decisive bearing on editorial decisions. Just as writing style and
diction change from era to era, so does orthography, albeit not so
drastically.[36] In the *Theorica musice,* such changes can be easily
recognized by comparing specimens from the text with entries
in standard Latin dictionaries. On the whole, Gaffurio's orthography conforms with medieval Latin usage which itself exhibits
considerable agreement with classical Latin. The miniscule *u*
(written as *V* in majuscule) is used for both the vocalic "u" as in
uno and the consonant "u" as in *ueteres*. Similarly, no distinction
is made between the vocalic "i" as in *igitur* and the consonant
"i" as in *Iosephus*. Common to medieval Latin is the doubling of
consonants, and we see this convention throughout the *Theorica
musice;* for instance, *apperire* instead of the classical *aperire*.
Also conventional in medieval Latin is the omission of the aspi-
ration; for instance, *nihil* instead of *nichil* and *armonica* instead
of *harmonica*.[37] In this regard, Gaffurio shows no consistency
in the usage of classical as opposed to medieval forms.

Another medieval characteristic is the displacement of the diphthongs *œ acuta* and *œ acuta* by *e caudata*. Again, Gaffurio is inconsistent, using now *que* and now *quae*. And since he frequently uses *que* as the relative pronoun, Gaffurio's language will seem ambiguous to the modern reader who is used to the classical distinction between *que*, the conjunction, and *quae*, the relative pronoun. Similar problems occur with the preposition *cum* and the conjunction *quom*.[38]

In view of the foregoing characteristics, the Latin in my critical edition has been standardized, that is, "classicized," in order to enhance its usefulness to the modern reader. This editorial decision requires the use of uniform orthography in the main body, with variants from the 1492 version reported in an accompanying table.[39] Standardization is also applied to such variants as *n* and *m*, *s* and *x*, *c* and *t*, *f* and *ph*, *t* and *ct*.

Another problem in fifteenth-century Latin is the fusion of patristic Latin with the contemporary, more vulgar Latin, and even with Italian.[40] Gaffurio includes Greek terms in latinized transliteration as well as Latin words supplied with Greek endings.[41] Though Gaffurio could not read Greek, his use of Greek terms respects a common tradition of the time, a tradition based on glossaries, bilingual Bibles, and such polyglot writers as Isidore of Seville.[42] My translation preserves this idiosyncrasy of Gaffurio's style.

Three categories of errors in the *Theorica musice* require emendations. The majority are mechanical, as in *nero* instead of *vero*. Grammatical mistakes are few; for instance, the confusion of *ab* and *ad*.[43] In the absence of manuscript versions of the treatise, the sources of these minor errors cannot be ascertained. Moreover, there are errors of a more substantial nature, including erroneous facts and faulty terminology; for example, the discussion of apotome and diesis.[44] All corrections, including those listed in the printer's *errata*,[45] are incorporated in the text, with the original readings provided in the footnotes.

Editors of fifteenth-century Latin texts are also confronted by abbreviations, commonly used in manuscripts and prints of this period. The printing of the *Theorica musice* cannot be taken as an indicator of the types of abbreviations used by Gaffurio when writing by hand. A partial collation of the 1480 and 1492 versions shows that neither the abbreviations themselves nor their placement are identical, suggesting that most of them were introduced in the process of typesetting. This hypothesis is substantiated by the observation that the number of abbreviations increases toward the end of lines and at the bottom of pages— evidence that their function was to ensure uniform alignment of words at the right margin of the page.

The abbreviations can be broken down into two types. Regular abbreviations are indicated generally by a single letter followed by a period; for example, *i.* for *idest.*[46] A substantially larger group incorporates signs of contraction, signs that signify the omission of one or more letters, or even a complete syllable, of a word. A special class in the latter group is the abbreviated form of verbs; for example, *declarasse* for *declaravisse.*[47] In my critical edition all abbreviations are resolved, with the resolution indicated by italicized type in the text.[48] The occasional wrong contraction sign in the original is given an emended resolution in the text and an explanation in the annotations.

Although the two printed versions show little consistency in the use of abbreviations, a comparison of specific words does indicate a less haphazard practice than might appear at first glance. In the case of *scilicet*, for example, the printer/author supplied the more common fourteenth-century abbreviation in the 1480 edition, whereas in the 1492 version the usual fifteenth-century abbreviation is invariably used.[49]

Another aid to proper alignment was the hyphenating of words. Frequently, though, hyphens are missing in the original. In my edition, their presence is assumed without annotations. Besides inconsistent hyphenation, the printer occasionally compacted words together in order to fit them into a single line.

Punctuation is a major problem in preparing modern editions of early sources, regardless of their transmission by manuscript or print. The exact reproduction of original punctuation would impede rather than enhance the comprehensibility of a critical edition. Nevertheless, editors should pay attention to original punctuation, insofar as it may guide them in deciphering the meaning of the text. In the case of the *Theorica musice* I have chosen to modernize the punctuation by deleting and adding symbols where necessary. Gaffurio employed three symbols: colon, period, and question mark. Whereas the latter two seem to function in the standard modern way, the colon often acts as our modern semicolon. Rather than clutter the footnotes with explanations of punctuation, editorial symbols are framed by square brackets. Deletions are effected tacitly, unless they contribute to the clarification of the text.

Closely associated with punctuation is the practice of capitalization, which has been altered without further comment to conform with modern usage. However, a few comments on this aspect of the *Theorica musice* are in order here. The most common use of capitalization is to mark the start of sentences, a use for which the modern editor can be grateful inasmuch as the printer frequently forgot to insert any punctuation at the end of sentences. In addition, capitals are used for emphasis either in enumerating things, distinguishing types, or calling attention to technical terms.[50] It must be said, however, that this usage is by no means consistent.

The absence of quotation marks in the *Theorica musice*, a trait shared with most printed documents from this and earlier periods, is a crucial issue for modern editors, for it contributes to the problem of identifying sources. Without such marks, it is not a simple matter to separate source citations from Gaffurio's own prose. I have supplied quotation marks within square brackets in my edition to indicate verbatim quotations or short *dicta*.

Medieval and renaissance documents, unlike modern writing, present a continuous unfolding of thought without recourse to

paragraphing. However, clues about paragraphs or topic group-
ings exist in the *Theorica musice* in the page layout and the prose
syntax, especially Gaffurio's use of conjunctions to mark new
thoughts. The insertion of tables, diagrams, and other illustra-
tions generally signals a break in the presentation, if not the end
of a topic, because these devices usually give a summary of what
has been said up to that point. The most common conjunctions
separating topics are *autem* and *item*. When used for this reason,
they are replaced in my edition by paragraphs; but when they
serve a grammatical function, they are of course translated into
the appropriate English equivalents.

THE SOURCES. The *Theorica musice* is truly encyclopedic in
scope, embracing many disciplines, such as music history, music theory, classical studies, theology, philosophy, mythology,
medicine, astronomy, physics, and mathematics. The many issues raised by Gaffurio require a broad knowledge of the literature in order to identify and trace particular currents of thought.
It is thus crucial to annotate carefully the sources of Gaffurio's
ideas.

When editing and translating a treatise like the *Theorica musice*, it is futile to pursue every reference. More important is the
tracing of sources to which Gaffurio was indebted for his theoretical thinking. At the same time, parallel or correlative passages
are identified, especially when they contribute to understanding
the subject matter at hand or when they illustrate commonplaces
in Gaffurio's thought. Many of Gaffurio's statements or ideas,
if judged solely in their context, seem to be gratuitous observations. As it turns out, these can be usually traced to a congeries
of sources. In the annotations to my edition the most likely
source is given first, with subsequent references arranged in the
order of their proximity to Gaffurio's enunciation. Since Gaffurio
relied on Latin sources or on Latin translations of Greek sources,
Latin documents take precedence over Greek.

The task of identifying sources is rendered more difficult by
Gaffurio's inconsistency in naming authors and treatises, a trait

endemic to humanist writers. Even when Gaffurio provides an author's name (in the text or margin), the source thus implied or even the attributed authorship may not yield a totally convincing solution to the transmission of a particular idea. For example, the account of the Stoic doctrine on hearing, ascribed to Apollodorus [of Athens],[51] comes from Diogenes Laertius's *Vitae philosophorum*.[52] Especially whenever a Greek author is listed, the link between the original source and Gaffurio requires documentation. For example, Gaffurio refers to Aristotle's *The Heavens and the Universe* (2.9.290B–291A); in all likelihood, the mediating source in this instance is Giorgio Anselmi's *Dialoghi* (f.5 verso).[53]

A further obstacle to locating borrowed material is Gaffurio's consistent prose style, his seamless writing that blurs the boundaries of subtexts. Considering the disparate source material in the *Theorica musice*, it is not surprising to discover that Gaffurio usually paraphrases his sources in the body of the discourse. And by presenting close series of paraphrases, he is able to assemble abundant material in relatively little space. Except for a lengthy passage from Anselmi's *De musica*, and some excerpts from Boethius,[54] literal quotations are reserved for poetry.[55]

A more detailed examination of the citations reveals that they may be grouped into several categories. At their most complete, references include author and source as well as book and/or chapter number; however, very few contain so much data.[56] As a rule, Gaffurio merely gives the author's name. This information suffices when, as is normally the case, the treatise can be determined from the context.[57] Occasionally, a reference to an author and treatise cannot be verified, for the simple reason that the source is no longer extant.[58] Such cases must be accepted unconditionally, a relatively unproblematic decision insofar as Gaffurio makes only three errors.[59] Sometimes, Gaffurio acknowledges his source in a sentence that comes after the pertinent quotation and introduces further paraphrased material.[60] Rarely does he not acknowledge his sources. The most substantial instance of "plagiarism" occurs in the opening chapter of Book I, a quarter of which is based on an unidentified translation of pseudo-Plutarch's *De musica*.[61] Although Plutarch's name later appears in a list of Greek authorities,[62] one must ask whether this casual reference is a sufficient acknowledgement for so lengthy a quotation.

Regardless of the state of completeness of the references in the *Theorica musice*, the annotations contain complete citations according to received format.[63] In several instances, the annotations furnish an opportunity to fill in incomplete information on sources or to help decodify the occasional cryptic remark in the text.[64]

THE PREPARATION OF THE TRANSLATION. My translation aims at an idiomatic English rendition in readable prose, one which remains faithful to the style of the original language. Mathiesen stresses the consistent treatment of vocabulary.[65] Although this goal has been pursued whenever possible, Gaffurio's use of words is such that it was necessary to modify Mathiesen's recommendation. Two aspects of Gaffurio's *Theorica musice* exemplify some of the problems and decisions that editors must face to capture the style of the original text in an elegant fashion.

Throughout his treatise Gaffurio strove to present the material in a lucid way, and to keep his syntax clear and his vocabulary varied. In some of the later chapters, especially in Book 5, this proved difficult because of the repetitiveness of the material and the need to describe in words information already available in diagrams. For example, in chapter 6 of Book 5, Gaffurio offers a painstaking exposition of Guido's distribution of letters and syllables, denoting the string divisions on the monochord. Though the facts remain the same, Gaffurio deliberately changes the verb in each sentence in an attempt to relieve monotony. Gaffurio's choice shows his imaginative and subtle command of the language; and my translation reflects his style by using English equivalents for the multitude of Latin verbs, all of which express a single idea.

The *Theorica musice* abounds in technical terms, and these pose a thorny problem in that their meaning is contextual. The translation of such words as *vox, sonus, tonus,* and *corda* warrant special attention. A number of scholars have studied the changing contexts and usages over time of this essentially medieval terminology.[66] Each scholar offers a different solution for translating these terms. And although none of them centers on the *Theorica musice*, their suggestions are relevant to the search for correct translations that suit the specific contexts within Gaffurio's treatise.

The first chapter of Book 5, which focuses on the Greek *systema teleion,* provides many examples of ambiguous terminology. The basic English renderings of *vox* as "voice," *sonus* as "sound," *tonus* as "tone," and *corda* as "string" would not convey the proper meaning. *Corda,* for instance, must be translated as "step" in the discussion of string divisions. Even though "voice" is a satisfactory translation of *vox* in terms of the properties of sound, as in Book 2, chapter 1, in other chapters, such as chapter 2 of Book 2, the proper translation is "pitch" in the sense of a sung tone. *Tonus* in Book 5, chapter 1 carries the ordinary meaning of the interval of a "whole tone." But in chapter 8 of the same book *tonus* is a synonym for *tropus* or *modus*; in this case, the appropriate English word is "mode."

Gaffurio used *sonus* in four different contexts, thus invoking four different meanings.[67] In Book 5, chapter 1 *sonus* seems to be a synonym for *tonus,* and hence must be translated as "tone." In chapter 2 of the same book *sonus* takes on the meaning of *corda,* hence "step." A little later the same term implies a written note. On the other hand, in Book 2, chapter 1 *sonus* clearly means "sound" as an acoustical phenomenon perceived by the ear.

Some translation problems have been sidestepped by avoiding literal adherence to the original wording, thus obviating the search for equivalents for every single Latin term. For one thing, idioms of speech may have penetrated written style.[68] Ignorance of this possibility can mislead translators into observing every conjunction and particle. Like other humanists of his time, Gaffurio often resorts to personal pronouns, such as declined forms of *ipse*. These may be disregarded, since they are not idiomatic to English and do not add to the understanding of a passage. At the same time, complex metaphorical language often requires repetitions and insertions to clarify the meaning in English, a language without noun declension and gender.[69]

IMPLEMENTATION. Let us examine how the guidelines outlined above can be implemented in a representative passage from Book 4, chapter 3, entitled "The Nature of Tones and Semitones," of Gaffurio's *Theorica musice*. The excerpt is presented in a reproduction of the 1492 print,[70] and below in the modern edition and the English translation.[71]

Example 1

[63] Quantoq*ue* semitonium minus recto toni dimidio minus est tanto apotome integrum toni dimidium excedit. [64] Et quoniam monstratum est semitonium inter 256 et 243 principaliter consistere, [64a] nunc in quibus maioribus numeris constet apotome discutie*n*dum est. [65] Si enim 243 octavam possent recipere partem ita ut ad eum suus posset sesquioctavus comparari, tunc 256 [66] habitudo ad ipsius minoris sesquioctavam collata apotomen necessaria ratione probaret. [67] Sed quoniam ipse 243 numerus octavam partem habere non potest [glv] singuli numeri octonario crescant; [68] *et* quidem 243 numerus octies ductus numerum 1944 perficit, [69] qui dum propria superponatur octava scilicet 243 mox fie*n*t 2187. [70] Ite*m* 256 numer*us* crescat octies numeru*m* 2048 co*n*ducet [,] [71] qui praeductoru*m* [71a] med[i]us collocetu*r* hoc mo*d*o [.]

Figure 4.3.2

[72] Tertius itaque terminus ad primum tonum ducit [72a] sesquioctava ratione comprehensum. [73] Secundus vero ad primum semitonium minus sed tertius ad secundum [73a] apotomen [74] idcirco quia in minoribus numeris maior evenit proportio et consequenter maior consonantia. [75] In maioribus autem minor.

[64a]: minoribus 1492, minimus 1480. Concerning the emendation in both versions, see the annotations to the Translation, in particular *Theorica musice* 4.3 [64a].

[69]: quibus 1492, 1480 (wrong relative pronoun).

[70]: 256 1492 (emendation of original "259;" see errata sheet included in the publication).

semitonium minus   apotome
1944   2048   2187   1480
sesquioctava proportio

Figure 4.3.2

[73]: apotomen 1492, semitonium minus 1480. Concerning the emendation in the *Theorica musice,* see the annotations to the Translation, in particular *Theorica musice* 4.3 [73].

[73a]: semitonium minus 1492, semitonium maius 1480 [semitonium maius is alternate terminology for apotomen]. Concerning the emendation in the *Theorica musice,* see the annotations to the Translation, in particular *Theorica musice* 4.3 [73a].

[75]: minoribus 1492; this emendation is necessitated by the interpretation of the preceding sentences (see *Theorica musice* 4.3 [64a] ff); also errata sheet included in the publication.

[63] By as much as the smaller semitone is smaller than the exact half of the tone, by so much the apotome exceeds the unimpaired half of the tone. [64] And since it has been shown that the semitone lies principally between 256 and 243, [64a] it must now be discussed in what larger numbers the apotome exists. [65] In fact, if 243 can accept an eighth part so that its sesquioctaval proportion can be compared with it, namely, 256, [66] this representation, having been placed in relation to the sesquioctaval proportion of this smaller number, would define the apotome by a necessary ratio. [67] But since this number 234 cannot have an eighth part [glv], let the individual numbers rise by the [factor] eight; [68] and certainly, the number 243, taken eight times, completes the number 1944, [69] to which if its own eighth [part], that is, 243, is now added, 2187 results. [70] Likewise, let the number 256, [taken] eight times, grow to 2048; [71] [this number] will bring together that [number] [71a] which is placed as the middle [number] of those previously discussed, as in Figure 4.3.2.

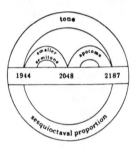

Figure 4.3.2

[72] The third term to the first produces the tone, [72a] comprehended by the sesquioctaval ratio. [73] The second term to the first produces the smaller semitone, and the third term to the second [73a] the apotome [74] for the reason that since the larger proportion occurs in the smaller numbers, the larger consonance consequently results; [75] the smaller proportion, on the other hand, occurs in the larger numbers.

---

[63]–[64]: Boethius *De institutione musica* 2.30.263.26–28, 264.1–2: *Quantum igitur semitonium minus integre dimidio toni minus est, tantum apotome toni integrum superat dimidium. Et quoniam docuimus*

semitonium in CCLVI et CCXLIII principaliter stare, nunc ea, quae apotome dicitur, . . . Gaffurio here obviously confused the terminology in both versions of the treatise: (. . . *in quibus minoribus numeris constet apothome* instead of the correct *nunc in quibus maioribus numeris constet apothome* . . .).

[64]: Gaffurio's discussion here as well as in the preceding sentences centers around the *semitonium minus* (also known as *limma* or *diesis*). The numbers 256 and 243 represent the ratio of the diesis; this proportion is arrived at through subtraction of two whole tones (ratio 9:8) from the interval of the diatessaron (ratio 4:3). Recalling that the subtraction of an interval is achieved through multiplication with its inverted fractions, we obtain:

$$\frac{4}{3} : \frac{9^2}{8} = \frac{4}{3} \times \frac{8^2}{9} = \frac{4}{3} \times \frac{64}{81} = \frac{256}{243}$$

[64a]: Gaffurio here has clearly confused the Pythagorean terminology. In both 1480 and 1492 editions Gaffurio equates the *apotome* with the *semitonium minus* (as becomes evident from his writing: *minoribus numeris* 1492; *minimus numeris* 1480). Yet the proportion which he provides in *Theorica musice* 4.3 [64] is that of the *diesis* (or *limma*) to the *semitonium minus*, but *not* of the *apotome* (see explanation to *Theorica musice* 4.3 [73]). The subsequent figure in the *Theoricum* identifies the *semitonium minus* and the *apotome* correctly.

[65]–[71a]: Boethius *De inst. mus.* 2.30.264.314.

[71]: That is, 1944, 2048, 2187.

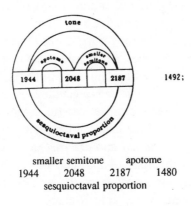

smaller semitone   apotome
1944   2048   2187   1480
sesquioctaval proportion

Figure 4.3.2

[72]: That is,

$$\frac{2187}{1944} = \frac{9}{8} : \frac{9}{8} \times 243 = \frac{2187}{1944}$$

Boethius *De inst. mus.* 2.30.264.15–16.

[72a]: This is Gaffurio's insertion for clarification of [72].

[73]: The *apotome* is defined as the difference between the whole tone (ratio 9:8) and the *semitonium minus* (or *diesis*) (ratio 256:243). Applying a mathematical operation similar to the one in *Theorica musice* 4.3 [64], we obtain:

$$\frac{9}{8} : \frac{256}{243} = \frac{9}{8} \times \frac{243}{256} = \frac{2187}{2048}$$

[73]–[73a]: Boethius *De inst. mus.* 2.30.264.16–17: *secundus vero ad primum semitonii minoris, apotomes vero tertius ad secundum.* Gaffurio confused the terminology in the *Theorica musice* (. . . *Secundus vero ad primum apothomen sed tertius ad secundum semitonium minus . . .* instead of the correct: *Secundus vero ad primum semitonium minus sed tertius ad secundum apothomen . . .*), whereas the *Theoricum* shows the correct identification of *apotome* and *diesis*.

[73a]: In Pythagorean terminology the *diesis* (*limma*) (ratio 243:256).

This passage presents a set of calculations underlying the process of continuous subtraction, known as *antanairesis*, a process that was fundamental in determining many of the intervals of the Pythagorean scale.[72] It includes a peculiar error in terminology. Gaffurio's reversal of ratios for the diesis (smaller semitone) and apotome (larger semitone), a confusion also evident in an earlier work,[73] was first noticed by Giovanni Spataro.[74]

Gaffurio's *Theorica musice* is a genuine exemplar of humanist scholarship. His effective prose, careful organization, and compelling presentation of the material bear witness to his thorough training in *ars grammatica* and *ars rhetorica*, a training which, like other music theorists of his day, he received early in his life.[75] The treatise is also one of the earliest music-theoretical documents, printed in movable Roman type, and thus typifies the state of music printing during the last two decades of the fifteenth century. In exploring how to make such a work accessible to the modern reader, this essay provides guidelines for unambiguous editing and intelligible translating. Thus, Gaffurio's *Theorica musice* may serve as a representative example of the earliest stage of music printing and the problems associated with this mode of text transmission for editors and translators.

NOTES

This paper is the result of many fruitful discussions with Professor Claude V. Palisca of Yale University, whom I thank for his many valuable comments and suggestions. I am grateful to Professors Claud A. Thompson and John W. Stephenson (Associate Deans of Humanities and Fine Arts, and Sciences, respectively), who nominated me for a grant from the College Research Fund, College of Arts and Science of the University of Saskatchewan. This grant supported the writing of the paper and the production of the plates. I wish also to thank Dr. M. A. Baird, Music Librarian of the University of London, and Professor Harold Samuel, Director of the Yale Music Library, as well as the staff of this Library, for making available to me copies of Gaffurio's treatises. I am also indebted to Professor John Rothgeb of SUNY at Binghamton for sending me a copy of *Translation Perspective: Selected Papers, 1982–83.*

1. Ed. C. V. Palisca (New Haven and London 1963–). Thirteen volumes so far.

2. Edd. T. J. Mathiesen and J. Solomon (Lincoln and London 1982–). Six volumes so far.

3. Lincoln and London 1982.

4. *Anicii Manlii Torquati Severini Boetii De institutione arithmetica libri duo, De institutione musica libri quinque, accedit geometriae quae fertur Boetii e libris manu scriptis* (Leipzig 1867).

5. W. K. Kreyszig "Franchino Gaffurio's *Theorica musice* (1492): Edition, Translation and Study of Sources" (Ph.D. diss. Yale University 1989). The translation, with introduction and annotations, appeared in 1993 as a volume in *Music Theory Translation Series [MTTS]* ed. Palisca.

6. One of the principal publishers of classical texts is B. G. Teubner. For an overview of Teubner's contributions, see R. Merkelbach "Die Altertumswissenschaft bei Teubner" *Wechselwirkungen: Der wissenschaftliche Verlag als Mittler* (Stuttgart 1986) 11–26.

7. For example, P. Gaskell *From Writer to Reader: Studies in Editorial Method* (Oxford 1978); M.-J. Kline *A Guide to Documentary Editing* (Baltimore and London 1987); G. L. Vogt and J. B. Jones edd. *Literary and Historical Editing* **University of Kansas Publications Library Series** 46 (University of Kansas Libraries 1981).

8. *Thesaurus Linguae Latinae*, centered in Munich and published by Teubner in Leipzig, concentrates largely on classical Latin literature. A similar focus characterizes *Thesaurus Linguae Graecae*. Both this project and the *Lexicon Musicum Latinum* are centered in Munich. On the objectives of the *Lexicon Musicum Latinum*, see H. Schmidt "Plan und Durchführung des 'Lexicon Musicum Latinum' I: Erfassung und Erforschung der musikalischen Fachsprache des Mittelalters" *Bericht über den Internationalen Musikwissenschaftlichen Kongress Kassel 1962* edd. G. Reichert and M. Just (Kassel 1963) 349–50; E. Waeltner "Plan und Durchführung des 'Lexicon Musicum Latinum' II: Archivaufbau mit Hilfe maschineller Datenverarbeitung" *Bericht . . . Kongress Kassel 1962* 351–2.

9. Centered at Indiana University in Bloomington, this project is headed by Mathiesen.

10. *Anicius Manlius Severinus Boethius: Fundamentals of Music* *MTTS* (New Haven and London 1989).

11. "Ein anonymer unvollständiger Musiktraktat des 15. Jahrhunderts in Philadelphia, U. S. A." *Kirchenmusikalisches Jahrbuch [KmJ]* 44 (1960) 27–44.

12. "Ein unvollständiger Musiktraktat des 14. Jahrhunderts in Ms. 1201 der Universitätsbibliothek Graz" *KmJ* 44 (1960) 14–27, "Ein anonymer Musiktraktat aus der 1. Hälfte des 16. Jahrhunderts in Cod. 514 der Benediktinerabtei Göttweig/Niederösterreich" *KmJ* 45 (1961) 58–81, and "Ein anonymer Musiktraktat aus der 2. Hälfte des 14. Jahrhunderts in der Stiftsbibliothek Michaelbeuren/Salzburg" *KmJ* 46 (1962) 43–60.

13. *The Lucidarium of Marchetto of Padua: A Critical Edition, Translation, and Commentary* (Chicago and London 1985), and *Prosdocimo de' Beldomandi: Contrapunctus (Counterpoint)* **Greek and Latin Music Theory** 1 edd. Mathiesen and Solomon (Lincoln and London 1984).

14. *Musica et Scolia enchiriadis una cum aliquibus tractaculis adiunctis* **Bayerische Akademie der Wissenschaften: Veröffentlichungen der Musikhistorischen Kommission** 3 (Munich 1981).

15. *Ugolino Urbeventanis: Declaratio musicae disciplinae* **Corpus Scriptorum de Musica** 7 ed. A. Carapetyan (Rome 1959–62).

16. Dedicated to Lodovico il Moro, Duke of Milan, and printed by the well established Filippo Mantegazza, with the cost of publication borne by Giovanni Petri di Lomazzo. A reproduction of the title page is provided in Plate III.

17. Dedicated to John Arcimboldi, Cardinal Bishop of Novara, and published by Franciscus di Dino Florentinus.

18. Published by Guilermus Signerre. Facsimile (Farnborough 1967). Trans. C. A. Miller *Franchino Gaffurius: Practica musicae* **Musicological Studies and Documents** [*MSD*] 20 ed. A. Carapetyan (American Institute of Musicology 1968). Trans. I. Young *The Practica musicae of Franchinus Gafurius* (Madison 1969).

19. Published by Gotardus Pontanus Calographus. Facsimile ed. G. Vecchi (Bologna 1972). Trans. Miller *Franchinus Gaffurius: De harmonia musicorum instrumentorum opus MSD* 33 (1977).

20. The *Theoricum opus musice discipline* is preserved in the manuscript Bologna: Civico Museo Bibliografico Musicale A 71; see K.-W. Gümpel "Das Enchiridion de principiis musice discipline des Guillermus de Podio" *Gesammelte Aufsätze zur Kulturgeschichte Spaniens* 27 (1973) 359–96. The *Practica musicae* is transmitted in a manuscript at Bergamo; see Miller "Early Gaffuriana: New Answer to Old Questions" *Musical Quarterly* 56 (1970) 367. *De harmonia musicorum* survives in manuscripts located in Lodi, Paris, Lyon, Naples, and Vienna; see Palisca *Humanism in Italian Renaissance Musical Thought* (New Haven and London 1985) 201–3.

21. For an overview of the location of these copies see Kreyszig "Franchino Gaffurio's *Theorica musice* (1492)" 36–7 (Appendix 2.2).

22. *Editing Greek and Latin Texts (Papers Given at the Twenty-Third Annual Conference on Editorial Problems, University of Toronto, 6–7 November 1987)* ed. J. Grant (New York 1989).

23. S. Dow *Conventions in Editing: A Suggested Reformulation of the Leiden System* **Greek, Roman, and Byzantine Scholarly Aids** 2 (Durham 1969).

24. Ed. G. Cesari (Rome 1934); **Monuments of Music and Music Literature in Facsimile—Second Series: Music Literature** 21 (New York 1967).

25. The collation of the 1492 copy at Yale University with the 1480 copy at the University of London is presented in a table in Kreyszig "Franchino Gaffurio's *Theorica musice* (1492)" 626–34.

26. For a detailed discussion of the collation of the two versions, see Kreyszig "Franchino Gaffurio's *Theorica musice* (1492)" 512–46.

27. See H. Harth "Probleme der Edition lateinischer Humanistentexte am Beispiel des Poggio-Briefwechsels" *Probleme der Edition mittel- und neulateinischer Texte: Kolloquium der Deutschen Forschungsgemeinschaft* edd. L. Hodl and D. Wattke (Boppard/Rhein 1978) 92.

28. *Textual Criticism and Editorial Technique Applicable to Greek and Latin Texts* (Stuttgart 1973).

29. On the classification of classical and medieval Latin, see A. G. Rigg "Medieval Latin" *Editing Medieval Texts English, French, and Latin Written in England (Papers Given at the Twelfth Annual Conference of Editorial Problems, University of Toronto, 5–6 November 1976)* ed. Rigg (New York and London 1977) 107–25.

30. See D. Williman "Translating Medieval Latin" *Translation Perspective: Selected Papers, 1982–83* ed. M. Gaddis Rose (Binghamton 1984) 57–62.

31. Palisca *Humanism* 23–50.

32. J. Ijsewijn "Mittelalterliches Latein und humanistisches Latein" *Die Rezeption der Antike: Zum Problem der Kontinuität zwischen Mittelalter und Renaissance* ed. A. Buck *Wolfenbütteler Abhandlungen zur Renaissanceforschung* 1 (Hamburg 1981) 71–83.

33. For examples of these elements, see Gaffurio *Theorica musice* 4.3 [26]–[27], 1.1 [228]–[229], 4.3 [31], 4.3 [51]–[53], 1.1 [65], *Prohemium* [32], [38].

34. F. Blatt "Sprachwandel im Latein des Mittelalters" *Historische Vierteljahrsschrift* 28 (1934) 41–52.

35. Horace *Ars poetica* 97 (*Theorica musice* 3.3 [42]); Ovid *Fasti* 6.663–67 (1.1 [129]–[131]); Augustine *De musica* 1.4.8 (1.5 [7a]–[11]); Boethius *De institutione musica* 1.1.185.3–4 (1.1 [81]); Isidore *Etymologiarum sive originum libri XX* 3.29, 13.1 (1.2 [4]); Anselmi *De musica* 1.149–50 (1.2 [11]–[13]); Marchetto *Lucidarium* 16 (1.5 [50]); Ficino *Timaeus* 47c-e (1.1 [202]-206]); Barbaro trans. of Themistius *Paraphraseos de anima libri tres* [Aristotle] 3 (1.5 [30]–[31]).

36.   On various orthographical changes in Latin, see K. Langosch *Lateinisches Mittelalter: Einführung in Sprache und Literatur* (Darmstadt 1975) 53–54; J. Marouzeau *Introduction au Latin Série Pédagogique* 4 (Paris 1970 3d ed.) 16; Blatt "Sprachwandel im Latein" 36–7; Williman "Translating Medieval Latin" 57.

37.   *Theorica musice* 1.1 [100], 3.5 [102], 1.1 [1], 1.1 [252], 1.1 [154], 4.2 [4], Figure 4.2.1.

38.   For example, *Theorica musice* 1.1 [49], 4.3 [79], [89].

39.   See Kreyszig "Franchino Gaffurio's *Theorica musice* (1492)" 1279–97. Such editorial practice follows Briner, Federhofer-Königs, Schmid, and Seay, rather than Mathiesen, who advocates faithfulness to the original.

40.   Harth "Probleme der Edition lateinischer Humanistentexte" 98. See Gaffurio *Angelicum ac divinum opus musice* (Milan 1508) 4.7.

41.   *Theorica musice* 1.4 [24]; 1.1 [29].

42.   Kreyszig "Franchino Gaffurio's *Theorica musice* (1492)" 32–3. See also O. Prinz "Zum Einfluss des Griechischen auf den Wortschatz des Mittellateins" *Festschrift Bernhard Bischoff zu seinem 65. Geburtstag* edd. J. Autenrieth and F. Brunhölzl (Stuttgart 1971) 1–15.

43.   *Theorica musice* 5.1 [9], 3.8 [12].

44.   *Theorica musice* 4.3 [73].

45.   *Theorica musice* folio 1 verso; see Plate IV.

46.   *Theorica musice* 3.5 [102]. A special type of abbreviation, the enclitic agglutination, uses the period to replace one or more letters, as in *.n.* for *enim*. See *Theorica musice* 1.2 [3].

47.   *Theorica musice* 1.1 [7].

48.   The resolutions are based on standard manuals and scholarly studies of paleography. For instance, A. Cappelli *Lexicon Abbreviaturarum Dizionario di Abbreviature latine ed italiane Manuale Hoepli* (Milan 1979); B. Bischoff *Paläographie des römischen Altertums und des abendländischen Mittelalters* **Grundlagen der Germanistik** 24 edd. H. Moser and H. Steinecke 2d rev ed (Berlin 1986).

49.   *Theoricum opus musice discipline* 2.5 line 43; *Theorica musice* 2.2 [117].

50.   For example, *Theorica musice* 1.6 [14], [16]; 5.5 [21]–[22]; 2.1 [16].

51.   *Theorica musice* 2.4 [1]–[3].

52. Diogenes Laertius *Vitae philosophorum* 7.158 (= *Stoicorum veterum fragmenta* 2.872.) I am indebted to Professor L. A. Holford-Strevens, of Oxford England, for this reference. See also Kreyszig *Franchino Gaffurio's Theorica musice (1492): A Study of the Sources* chap. 6 sec. 7 (in preparation).

53. *Theorica musice* 1.2 [8c]. On Anselmi as a source, see J. Haar "*Musica mundana:* Variations on a Pythagorean Theme" (Ph.D. diss. Harvard University 1960) 366.

54. See respectively, *Theorica musice* 1.1 [162]–[194] and 3.5 [92a]–[94]; 3.6 [63]–[65].

55. *Theorica musice* 1.1 [62], [72], [110]–[114], [128]–[129], [133]–[134], [137]–[140], and so on.

56. For example, the reference to the second book of Aristotle's *The Heavens and the Universe* mentioned above; see also *n* 53.

57. For example, Censorinus *De die natali ad Q. Caerellium* in *Theorica musice* 1.3 [25]–[26], [33]–[35], [37]–[67]. Gaffurio mentions only the author's name at 1.3 [37].

58. Such is the case with Varro's *Hebdomadibus vel de imaginibus,* cited in *Theorica musice* 5.1 [15a]–[20].

59. In *Theorica musice* 3.3 [40] Gaffurio confuses Varro and Cato by referring to Varro's books on agriculture; the citation is from Varro *De re rustica* 1.42, not Cato *De agricultura.* At 2.3 [35] Gaffurio mistakenly attributes the definition of *symphonia* to Augustine; for more details on the transmission of this misinformation, see W. R. Bowen "St. Augustine in Medieval and Renaissance Musical Science" *Augustine on Music: An Interdisciplinary Collection of Essays* ed. R. R. LaCroix *Studies in the History and Interpretation of Music* 6(Lewiston and Queenston 1988) 38, 50. At 2.3 [36] Gaffurio wrongly attributes a definition of harmonia to Hucbald, perhaps because he thought that Hucbald wrote the *Musica enchiriadis.* Incidentally, the statements about *symphonia* and *harmonia* can be found in Marchetto da Padua *Lucidarium in arte musice plane* 5.4–5; see Herlinger *The Lucidarium of Marchetto of Padua* 204–5.

60. For example, Cassiodorus *Varia* 2.40. 60–65, 94–103 in *Theorica musice* 1.1 [73]–[78].

61. *Theorica musice* 1.1 [3]–[18], [21]–[26], [30]–[33], [36]–[41], [51]–[52].

62. *Theorica musice* 1.1 [280].

63. Even when Gaffurio's references are exact and accurate, I have checked them against concordances and indices, standard and specialized dictionaries, and learned articles.

64. For example, *Theorica musice* 2.2 [116]–[119].

65. *A Style Guide for Text Criticism* 13.

66. M. Appel *Terminologie in den mittelalterlichen Musiktraktaten: Ein Beitrag zur musikalischen Elementarlehre des Mittelalters* (Bottrop 1935); H. P. Gysin *Studien zum Vokabular der Musiktheorie im Mittelalter: Eine linguistische Analyse* (Amsterdam 1958); H. H. Eggebrecht *Handwörterbuch der musikalischen Terminologie* (Wiesbaden 1972-).

67. For a comprehensive coverage of this term, see Eggebrecht and F. Reckow "Sonus" *Archiv für Musikwissenschaft [AfMw]* 25 (1968) 271–7.

68. Williman "Translating Medieval Latin" 58.

69. For example, *Theorica musice* 2.2 [72]–[74].

70. Plates V–VI.

71. From Kreyszig "Franchino Gaffurio's *Theorica musice* (1492)" 854–7, 1175–78.

72. C. A. Barbera "Pythagorean scale" *The New Harvard Dictionary of Music* ed. D. M. Randel (Cambridge 1986) 673.

73. Gaffurio *Theoricum opus musice discipline* 4.3 lines 117–22, corresponding to *Theorica musice* 4.3 [63]–[64a].

74. *Errori de Franchino Gafurio da Lodi da Maestro Joanne Spatario Musico Bolognese in sua defensione e del suo precettore Maestro Bartolomeo Ramis Hispano subtilimente demonstrati* (Bologna 1521). This book was written in the course of an intricate dispute about the mathematical definition of intervals. See H. Hüschen "Kritik und Polemik in der Musiktheorie des 15. Jahrhunderts" *Festschrift Arno Forchert zum 65. Geburtstag am 29. Dezember 1985* edd. G. Allroggen and D. Altenburg (Kassel 1986) 41–7.

75. J. Smits van Waesberghe "Studien über das Lesen (pronuntiare), das Zitieren und die Herausgabe lateinischer musiktheoretischer Traktate (9.–16. Jh.)" *AfMw* 29 (1972) 82.

The Translator as Interpreter:
Euclid's *Sectio canonis* and
Ptolemy's *Harmonica* in the Latin Tradition

Alan C. Bowen

Institute for Research in Classical Philosophy and Science

and William R. Bowen

University of Toronto

INTRODUCTION. To say that a translator is an interpreter is to say that to translate a text you must understand it, and that to understand it you must interpret it, that is, adapt it interactively with your own views of the subject. Such a claim raises numerous questions about translation and interpretation that fall today under the general rubric of hermeneutics. But it is also a claim of interest for the historical study of how ideas are transmitted from one culture to another. So, in what follows, we propose to bypass such hermeneutical worries as whether translation so described is possible, or what it means to maintain this. Instead, we shall analyze instances of translation in the pre-modern period.

One of the important features of the emergence of the modern era by the seventeenth and eighteenth centuries is the gap it created between later and earlier thinkers. The factors involved in producing this gap are numerous and complicated; but its consequences are, for our purposes at least, quite simple. For this gap separates modern thinkers from the community of thought that had existed previously among those on the other side of it. No longer may interpreters assume without question that they are somehow in conversation with Plato (429–347 BC), for instance. Or to put it even more sharply, no longer is it acceptable simply to profess being a Platonist in the way that pre-modern thinkers did. One of the many reasons for this is that the modern understanding of the universe as a system subject to a single set of physical laws involves a profound break with previous thought, since it had been the custom to treat the cosmos as divided into domains or regions to be studied and explained differently. This break, then, is not like the disagreements that existed between theories that competed previously for a thinker's allegiance, because, for all their purported divergences, they were in reality members of the same family—they stood in a fairly direct evolutionary line as heirs to the views of the ancients. Today no interpreter is permitted to do without question what he could have done before the modern era, that is, to claim simply as his own some version of the ancient cosmology and content himself with tinkering with its details. Were this his goal, to be credible he would first have to offer an *apologia* for the superiority of the view he professes to the modern conception.

In other words, with the beginning of the modern era, the world as it was conceived before is no longer the only alternative. Indeed, it is now not even the main alternative. The pre-modern world-view is no longer available to tacit assumption in its broad outlines, but has instead become an object for thorough criticism in a new way. And one of the new disciplines for the critical study of how this world-view as expressed in Greek and Latin literature is classical philology. But what, then, is translation before philology, before the critical study of ancient literature with its attendant specification of standards for the proper rendering of one language in another? What is translation in a period when the interactive adaptation of the original to one's own grasp of the subject-matter was unencumbered by modern requirements of accuracy and fidelity?

There is, of course, no reason to suppose that this question has only one answer; in truth, there may be at least as many answers as translators. Still one may presume that some works were translated in the pre-modern era because they promised support for a contemporary view. By itself such a motive would be unexceptionable as a context for translation at any time, of course. The problem arises, however, when the translator's interest in a text for the support it is thought to give for some theory collides with his own understanding of the theory. In such cases, the question is, How should one render the text when the claims made in it are at odds with the views it is expected to endorse? Nowadays, any answer to this question would be constrained by modern philological standards of accuracy and the related effort to distinguish (so far as possible) the translation of a work from its interpretation. But, in the pre-modern period the situation is different: though, as we will show, several ways of translating a text were recognized, these were not so narrowly specified that a translation could not become so interpretive as to transgress the limits of what would be accepted today as such.

Consequently, those interested in the transmission of ancient documents will find it instructive to compare pre-modern translations with the originals. For, by this comparison, they may discern how the documents translated were read and understood, and also discover reasons for the course of their later history. So the divergences between the original and its pre-modern translation should not be dismissed summarily by appeal to modern standards of accuracy—there is, after all, little gained in rejecting all early translations as inept when they depart from the original. Nor should such divergences be obliterated by supposing that the translation is not based on a text now extant but rather represents accurately a (corrupt) textual tradition which has not survived. To the contrary, we propose that these divergences be examined carefully; for, as in the instances we are about to examine, they may prove to be signs of the adaptation of the original to the requirements of the theory it was intended to support.

In what follows we focus on the works of Boethius. We choose Boethius (*ca.* 480–524) because he was extremely influential in transmitting Greek learning to the Latin world. His major philosophical work, the *De consolatione philosophiæ*, was a standard text for discussion and inspiration throughout the Middle Ages; and his five theological tractates and his minor works—translations and commentaries on treatises by Aristotle, Cicero, and Porphyry, as well as purportedly independent works on logic—influenced medieval thought profoundly. Indeed, though the much repeated claim that one of Boethius' goals was to carry on and bring to completion the task started by Cicero some 500 years earlier, that is, to renew philosophical learning in Latin, may not in fact be true, it is undeniable that his efforts did have this consequence.[1]

For our interests, it is important that Boethius also wrote on non-philosophical subjects which he regarded as necessary preliminaries in the education of philosophers. Of his textbooks on the subjects of the quadrivium, those on *arithmetica*[2] and music theory enjoyed illustrious careers in the schools and have survived to this day.[3] Since Boethius' work on music theory, the *De institutione musica*, renders in Latin two important texts in Greek musical theory, Euclid's *Sectio canonis* and Ptolemy's *Harmonica*, we focus on it to determine what light these translations shed on the problem of characterizing the project of translation in the pre-modern era.

BOETHIUS AS A TRANSLATOR. We begin by considering what Boethius actually says about his practice as a translator. In the preface to his *De institutione arithmetica*, Boethius writes:

> *At non alterius obnoxius institutis artissima memet ipse translationis lege constringo, sed paululum liberius evagatus alieno itineri, non vestigiis, insisto. Nam et ea, quæ de numeris a Nicomacho diffusius disputata sunt, moderata brevitate collegi et quæ transcursa velocius angustiorem intellegentiæ præstabant aditum*

*mediocri adiectione reseravi, ut aliquando ad evidentiam rerum
nostris etiam formulis ac descriptionibus uteremur.*[4]

But I do not confine myself as a slave to the teachings of another by the strictest rule of translation; but having wandered
somewhat more freely, I tread on another's path, not in his
footsteps. For in fact, those matters concerning numbers which
Nicomachus discusses at rather great length, I have brought together with a measure of brevity; and those matters run through
more quickly which offer to understanding a rather narrow access, I have made accessible by small addition, so that to make
things evident we sometimes also use paradigms and diagrams.

In this passage Boethius appears to differentiate two methods of
translation. The first adheres strictly to the words of the text, in
order to represent faithfully in Latin the words, here likened to
footsteps, of the Greek original. The second is not concerned
with this sort of verbal fidelity: its goal is to represent the sense,
here likened to the path, of the original; and so it tolerates considerable freedom in how this is done. Both methods of translation were well established in medieval times. For example,
when Greek literary documents came to the attention of Islamic
scholars, they discriminated and debated the relative merits of
translations in which each Greek word received an Arabic equivalent and those in which the meaning of each Greek sentence
was captured by a sentence in Arabic without regard for verbal
correspondence.[5]

Boethius declares his preference for the second mode of translation.[6] Granted, one may hesitate to assume that Boethius' remarks in the preface to his translation of Nicomachus' *Introductio arithmetica* will apply to his translation(s) in the *De institutione musica*. Still, what he states in the *De institutione arithmetica* describes rather well, we think, his handling of the *Sectio
canonis* and the *Harmonica* in his musical treatise. There are
significant differences, however, in Boethius' translations of the
Greek arithmetical and musical works. In our view, the ultimate

cause of them, is that harmonic science, unlike *arithmetica*, has opposed schools of thought. Thus, given that the path he follows in *arithmetica* and harmonic science is Pythagorean,[7] Boethius' task in rendering the treatises by Euclid and Ptolemy was more challenging, as his translations show: for, as we will argue, his Latin versions depart in interesting ways from the Greek originals when they stray from his own vision of the proper path.

In any event, we are not persuaded by Calvin Bower's thesis that Boethius' translation of the *Sectio canonis* is not made directly from this treatise but from an *Introductio musica* written by Nicomachus of Gerasa sometime in the second century AD, a text no longer extant.[8] Though this is doubtless possible, there are problems in Bower's arguments that this work by Nicomachus ever existed or that it was used by Boethius. Now is not the occasion, however, to scrutinize Bower's case: this would require close study of the passages in the *De institutione musica* which Bower adduces and which, in our view, he sometimes misinterprets because he misses the sense of the Greek originals. What we can do in what follows is to make it clear that Boethius' practice as a translator is consistent with what he actually says and, hence, that there is no need to explain his departures from the Greek originals by positing that he is translating accurately some intermediary Greek text (no longer extant and nowhere else attested unambiguously) which already contains these deviations. At the same time, our remarks will serve to exonerate Boethius of the charge that his translations are inferior because his command of Greek was poor.[9]

BOETHIUS AND PTOLEMY'S *HARMONICA*. Our analysis begins with a study of how Boethius renders Ptolemy's *Harmonica* in Latin, and will proceed in three broad stages. First, we review the evidence for knowledge of Ptolemy's musical treatise in the Latin world before Boethius, in order to clarify Boethius' role as transmitter of Ptolemy's ideas. Then, we examine passages in which Boethius translates from the *Harmonica*. In particular, we concentrate on those chapters of the *De institutione musica* in which Boethius presents Ptolemy's epistemological account of harmonic science and of how it obtains the sort of knowledge peculiar to it. And, finally, we consider what consequences Boethius' version may have had for the reception of Ptolemy's views among Latin readers in the Middle Ages.

THE HISTORY OF THE *HARMONICA* TO BOETHIUS. According to G. J. Toomer, one may infer that since the *Harmonica* lacks a dedication, it was one of Ptolemy's latest works.[10] The earliest allusion in Greek to this treatise occurs in the *Excerpta e Nicomacho*, a compilation of passages purportedly taken from the writings of Nicomachus of Gerasa, who lived in the second century AD.[11] More than a century after Ptolemy (*ca.* 100–*ca.* 170), the *Harmonica* was made the subject of a diffuse commentary by Porphyry (232–*ca.* 305), a pupil of the philosopher, Plotinus (205–270). Porphyry's work is not a unified treatise but a text in the scholia-tradition: one of its values is the information it gives about authors and works many of which are not known otherwise.[12]

The earliest evidence of the *Harmonica* in the Latin world comes from the late fourth and early fifth centuries. Macrobius, in the course of explaining why it is thought that Mars and Saturn are maleficent but Venus and Jupiter beneficent, mentions the *Harmonica* and reports views stated in *Harm.* 1.7 and 3.16.[13] The problem here is the difficulty of determining whether Macrobius' access to the *Harmonica* was direct or indirect, by way of Porphyry, for example.[14] From the early sixth century comes book 5 of Boethius' *De institutione musica*. This is the first extant translation into Latin of an extended passage from Ptolemy's musical treatise. Indeed, though this book is incomplete and breaks off after nineteen chapters—with the headings for another eleven chapters listed in some manuscripts—it is possible that *De inst. mus.* 5 was intended to follow book 1 of Ptolemy's *Harmonica*.[15]

On the basis of this evidence for knowledge in the Latin world of Ptolemy's views in the *Harmonica*, one would rightly conclude that the indisputable influence of Boethius' writings on later generations, when coupled with the fact that his version of Ptolemy's thought was, apparently, uncontested by any rival translations, makes him a central figure in the transmission of Ptolemy's science of music to the Latin world. But there is a twist to the story. Much of what Boethius translates from the *Harmonica* and all that he takes from the *Sectio canonis* is unattributed in the *De institutione musica* to the original authors. This is not surprising. In general, translation is appropriation: it is a way of making one's own the views of another. Hence, for Boethius, who was writing at a time when there were none of the modern scruples about acknowledging sources, perhaps the question should not be Why does Boethius fail to acknowledge Ptolemy and Euclid as his sources?, but rather What is the significance of the attributions he actually does make?[16]

THE CHALLENGE OF PTOLEMY'S *HARMONICA*. When he comes to book 5 of the *De institutione musica*, Boethius announces in chapter 1 his intention to turn from his account of the division of the *canon* in book 4 to the points of disagreement among musical scholars (*musicæ doctores*). In other words, he is now going to examine the theoretical basis for the disputes among the various competing schools of musical thought. Thus, chapter 2 opens with the question, What is the nature (*vis*) of harmonic science?, an issue he has postponed until now. And from here to the end of chapter 3, he presents a version of Ptolemy's remarks about the so-called criteria of harmonic science in *Harm.* 1.1–2.

Overall, it is clear that Boethius has abridged Ptolemy's text. Yet what Boethius offers is, we will show, consistent with the sort of translation he promised in the *De institutione arithmetica*. Consequently, one should hesitate to suppose that it is a bad translation or that Boethius has failed to understand the original or, even less, that it is a good translation based on a textual tradition that has not survived.[17] To look at Boethius' text in any of these ways is, as we have already indicated, to miss the point by assuming the wrong categories of criticism. Instead, one should view Boethius' translations as an exercise in appropriation. But, if one does this, it is clear that Ptolemy's *Harmonica* would pose a problem for Boethius: the account of the criteria and the attendant criticism of the main schools of harmonic science simply do not fit with Boethius' commitment to one of these schools, the Pythagorean. So, lacking even the suspicion of modern philology, Boethius apparently did not set out to fill chapters 2 and 3 with a translation of Ptolemy's Greek which one is entitled now to criticize using the same rules as one would in assessing Bower's translation of Boethius' Latin. Instead, Boethius offered a translation which adopts Ptolemy's text to his own concerns, a translation that approaches and departs from the original in significant ways both linguistic and philosophical.

In order to explain the differences between Ptolemy's *Harm.* 1.1–2 and Boethius' *De inst. mus.* 5.2–3, we will need in the first place to understand Ptolemy's remarks about the criteria of harmonic science and of how the various schools of harmonic science differ in using them.

PTOLEMY ON HEARING AND REASON IN HARMONIC SCIENCE.[18] In the first two chapters of his *Harmonica* Ptolemy turns to what had become a prominent subject in contemporary intellectual circles, the question of the criterion of truth (κριτήριον τῆς ἀληθείας).[19] By Ptolemy's time the problem defining the context for accounts of the criterion was twofold: to explain the contributions of reason and sense-perception to knowledge of external objects, and to determine what infallible means there are for distinguishing particular truths about these objects from falsehoods.[20] The *Harmonica* tackles this problem in the limited domain of music; it focuses on the question of the criteria of truth or reality in the domain of music, that is, on the criteria of ἁρμονία.[21]

According to Ptolemy "harmonic science (ἁρμονική) is a capacity to apprehend (δύναμις καταληπτική) intervals of high and low pitch among sounds,"[22] and there are two faculties that serve as criteria of ἁρμονία—the sense of hearing (ἀκοή) and reason (λόγος). In other words, harmonic science is a branch of

knowledge by which one is able to account systematically for
intervals among pitches and to determine their ἁρμονία or tune-
fulness, i.e., the way pitches should or do fit together properly.
In obtaining and exercising this knowledge, however, one relies
on two faculties, hearing and reason.[23] Now, for Ptolemy, these
two faculties are criteria in different ways: as he says, "hearing
is (a criterion) as matter and experience; but reason, as form and
explanation."[24] To explain why hearing and reason are united
in this way in developing or using harmonic science, Ptolemy
first points out that in general it is characteristic of the senses
(αἰσθήσεις) to discover what is similar (τὸ σύνεγγυς) and to
admit from elsewhere what is accurate (τὸ ἀκριβές); but of reason to discover what is accurate and to receive from elsewhere
what is similar. For, he continues, "since matter is defined and
delimited alone by form and experience by the explanation of
motions, and since matter and experience are proper to sense-
perception but form and explanation to reason, it follows reason-
ably that the apprehensions (διαλήψεις) of the senses are defined
and delimited by the apprehensions of reason."[25] In short, hearing supplies the matter of (scientific) musical judgment and reason, the form. He then re-presents this subordination of hearing
to reason by adding that, "at least in the case of things known
through the sense-perception,"[26] it consists in "the apprehensions
of the senses first submitting their crudely grasped distinctions
to the apprehensions of reason and being guided by them to
distinctions which are accurate and coherent (ὁμολογουμέναι)."
This follows, he says, "because it happens that reason is simple, unmixed, and thus, complete in itself (αὐτοτελής), fixed
(τεταγμένος), and always the same in relation to the same things;
but that sense-perception is always involved with matter which
is confused and in flux."[27] Moreover, he adds, this has the result
that "because of matter's instability, neither the sense-perception
of all people nor even that of the same people is ever observed to
be the same in relation to objects similarly disposed, but needs
the further instruction of reason as a kind of cane."[28]

But if hearing is subject to error and relies on reason to make its reports accurate and part of a system of knowledge, Ptolemy is quick to qualify this in three ways.[29] First, he suggests that hearing may be brought to recognize its errors by reason; that is, that the apprehensions of hearing are corrigible. Next, he proposes that what hearing presents to reason does not always need correction. Finally, he allows that even when the individual apprehensions of hearing do not seem to require correction by reason, there may be imperceptible error and, under certain circumstances, this error may accumulate and become perceptible. These points are important and require comment.

Ptolemy presents the claim that hearing may be brought to recognize its errors by reason in an analogy:

> just as the circle drawn by eye alone often seems to be accurate until the circle made by reason brings [the eye] to the recognition of one that is really accurate, so, when some definite interval (διαφορά) between sounds is ascertained, it will initially seem sometimes neither to fall short of nor exceed what is appropriate, but is often exposed as not being so when the [interval] selected according to the proper ratio is compared, since hearing recognizes by the comparison the more accurate [one] as something genuine, as it were, beside that counterfeit.[30]

This clearly does not mean, as Barker supposes, that hearing alone can detect its unreliability.[31] Rather, the point is that, when on the strength of theory reason discovers an error in what hearing reports, reason must produce in sound what is correct (i.e., an interval defined by the proper ratio) so that hearing may apprehend it and acknowledge the error. This entails, of course, that reason equip itself with an instrument which it can employ in a way consistent with theory—a point to which we will return. In any case, Ptolemy clearly holds that both reason and hearing can detect errors in the apprehensions of hearing.[32]

Next, Ptolemy introduces the premise that it is in general easier to judge something than it is to do it; and then he concludes that this sort of deficiency of sense-perceptions does not miss the truth by much in the case of [our] recognizing whether there is or is not a simple difference between them nor, again, in the case of [our] observing the amounts of the differences at least when [the amounts] are taken in greater parts of the things to which they belong.[33]

The argument here is compressed. Ptolemy has just set forth an analogy in which hearing is said to err on many occasions when it alone is the basis of intoning an interval. So the premiss that it is easier to judge than it is to do something means, in particular, that hearing will have better results when it judges intervals that are intoned. In other words, hearing will prove more reliable in recognizing that a melody is out of tune than in producing the melody by means of some instrument such as the voice. But it does not follow from this sort of deficiency that the apprehensions of hearing and the other senses are always wrong. Nor does it follow that the senses are deficient as faculties in obtaining and exercising knowledge because they depend on reason to make their apprehensions scientific, and that what the senses apprehend and must submit to reason is always in error. For, as Ptolemy would have it, hearing "does not miss the truth by much" in discerning the mere occurrence of an interval between sounds or when it reports the amount of this interval (providing that this amount is suitably large). Now, the phrase 'does not miss the truth by much' is, we think, an instance of what the grammarians call *litotes*.[34] In short, Ptolemy means that under these circumstances hearing does not miss the truth at all,[35] and, thus, that the apprehensions of hearing, like those of any other sense, may in fact be correct and accurate (albeit not yet scientific).[36]

This brings us to the claim that when hearing reports the amounts of intervals, in may often fail to discern the occurrence of error. As Ptolemy says of the senses in general,[37] if the amounts of the differences they apprehend are a relatively small part of the things exhibiting them, the senses may not discern any difference at all; yet, when such apprehensions are iterated, the error or difference accumulates and eventually becomes perceptible. In the case of hearing, for example, this may happen when hearing intones a sequence of intervals in a melody by means of the voice, that is, in singing.

Thus, the relation of reason and the senses in obtaining and exercising scientific knowledge is complex. In general, what the senses apprehend or report can become scientific only when integrated by reason into an explanatory system.[38] Now, if reason on taking recourse to theory discovers that the apprehensions of the senses are not accurate or if the senses discover a difference where there should be none, reason must ascertain the truth and offer correction. And it does this for hearing by means of some rational procedure (τινος ἀπὸ τοῦ λόγου ἐφόδου) against which, in Ptolemy's words, "the apprehensions of hearing will not testify but to which they will agree."[39] As we have said, this procedure must not only be consistent with the requirements of theory, but it must also be such that hearing will in principle acknowledge *and assent to its applications.* For only by such a procedure will reason be able to correct hearing by producing for its apprehension intervals among sounds that are accurate. In short, Ptolemy requires the production "of a rational criterion through proper instruments" (κριτηρίου λογικοῦ διὰ τῶν οἰκείων ὀργάνων).

But what is this rational criterion and what is the instrument? Ptolemy begins with the instrument.[40] He identifies it as the harmonic *canon* or ruler,[41] adding that the name is taken from common usage and from its straightening (κανονίζειν) things in the senses that fall short regarding truth. Next, Ptolemy asserts that

it should be the aim of the harmonic theorist to maintain in every way the rational [arithmetical] models (ὑποθέσεις)[42] of the *canon* as never conflicting in any way with the senses in the judgment (ὑπόληψις) of most people, just as, it should be the astronomer's aim to maintain the [geometrical] models (ὑποθέσεις) of the celestial motions as concordant with their observed periods, models that have themselves been taken from obvious and rather crude phenomena but find things accurately in detail through reason so far as it is possible.[43]

It turns out, then, that the third criterion, which is to serve as a means of distinguishing truth from falsehood in musical sound, is, in fact, the majority judgment about what is heard when the *canon* is properly set up according to theory and actually struck.[44]

We may now reflect on why Ptolemy allows that hearing does on occasion apprehend the truth and what this means. First, Ptolemy's criterion of the judgment made by the majority about what it hears when the *canon* is set up according to theory and sounded, requires not only, as we have said, that hearing be capable of apprehending true differences among sounds, but also that the judgment based on this apprehension be infallible, a thesis Ptolemy advances at *De iud. fac.* 11.1–2, when he maintains that (theoretical) reason by nature always tells the truth about its proper objects, "the same and different, the equal and unequal, the like and unlike, and in general the differences and similarities of kinds," Furthermore, the formulation of this criterion indicates that Ptolemy regards the phenomenon to be explained by harmonic science, ἁρμονία, as cultural, that is, as something defined in relation to the musical sensibilities or tastes of a community. In maintaining this, we are taking the phrase κατὰ τὴν τῶν πλείστων ὑπόληψιν, to mean "in the opinion of most people" and not just "in the opinion of most experts." Our reason is that there is no evidence for such a restriction in Ptolemy's preceding remarks and that our reading fits Ptolemy's comparison with astronomy better. Still, this restriction would affect our point only by limiting the scope of "community": for, in either case, questions about the sizes of melodic intervals concern matters of tuning and so inevitably involve the sense of what is musical. In this respect, harmonic science is unlike astronomy, since, as Ptolemy would presumably have it, the motions of the heavenly bodies are not as such subjective or dependent on human perception. At the same time, the qualification, "as heard by most people," is a check against the sort of scepticism that may arise about claims that harmonic science does in fact constitute knowledge of this cultural phenomenon, because of the acknowledged variations in hearing from person to person, and so on.[45]

Second, since harmonic science like any other science, if not always in progress, does have a period of development, it follows that its ὑποθέσεις or arithmetic models will require adjustment. But such adjustment is possible only if hearing can guide it. Yet hearing can guide it only if it is capable of apprehending and reporting correctly certain kinds of quantitative differences among sounds. Granted, it turns out that the hearing in question is that of the greatest number of people. Still, the point is important and it underlies the fact that the third criterion is a theoretically justified interval among sounds that the majority hears and assents to as correct. Accordingly, there is, if you will, a tension here between reason and hearing, a tension essential to Ptolemy's understanding of what harmonic science is: for, it would follow that as the musical sensibilities of the community change, the judgment of the majority about the size of melodic intervals will change and come to contradict conclusions of theory as manifested on the *canon*, with the result that the science of music itself must also change to keep pace.[46]

Ptolemy completes his remarks about the third criterion by attacking two rival schools for not paying attention to the proper aim of the harmonic theorist.[47] As he sees it, the first, the Pythagorean, addresses this aim too theoretically, "since the Pythagoreans do not even follow the application of hearing in the matters in which it is necessary for everyone, and to intervals among sounds they fit ratios inappropriate for many reasons to what is evident (τὸ φαινόμενον)."[48] In contrast, the second school, the Aristoxenian, seems to ignore the theorist's proper aim entirely, since its members hold only to the use of technical dexterity and the unadorned and irrational practice of sense:

> they give the greatest emphasis to things apprehended by sense and use reason as an incidental of their system—which is contrary to reason and contrary to what is evident: contrary to reason because they fit numbers, that is, the [numerical] representations of the ratios, not to the intervals of sounds but to the distances (διαστήματα) between them; and contrary to what is evident because they also apply these numbers in roles (μερισμοί) alien to the affirmations (συγκαταθέσεις) of the senses.

BOETHIUS' TRANSMISSION OF PTOLEMY'S VIEWS. To see how Boethius renders Ptolemy's account of the criteria of harmonic science, let us compare the first few sentences of *Harm.* 1.1 with Boethius' version of them in *De inst. mus.* 5.2.

Ptolemy, *Harm.* 1.1 Düring 3.1–8

Ἁρμονική ἐστι δύναμις καταληπτικὴ τῶν ἐν τοῖς ψόφοις περὶ τὸ ὀξὺ καὶ τὸ βαρὺ διαφορῶν, ψόφος δὲ πάθος ἀέρος πλησσομένου —τὸ πρῶτον καὶ γενικώτατον τῶν ἀκουστῶν—καὶ κριτήρια μὲν ἁρμονίας ἀκοὴ καὶ λόγος, οὐ κατὰ τὸν αὐτὸν δὲ τρόπον, ἀλλ' ἡ μὲν ἀκοὴ παρὰ τὴν ὕλην καὶ τὸ πάθος, ὁ δὲ λόγος παρὰ τὸ εἶδος καὶ τὸ αἴτιον, ὅτι καὶ καθόλου τῶν μὲν αἰσθήσεων ἴδιόν ἐστι τὸ τοῦ μὲν σύνεγγυς εὑρετικόν, τοῦ δὲ ἀκριβοῦς παραδεκτικόν, τοῦ δὲ λόγου τὸ τοῦ μὲν σύνεγγυς παραδεκτικόν, τοῦ δὲ ἀκριβοῦς εὑρετικόν.

Harmonic science is a capacity to apprehend intervals of high and low pitch among sounds; sound is a condition of air that is struck—it is the first and most general thing heard—and hearing and reason are criteria of *harmonia*, but not in the same way. Rather, hearing [is a criterion] as matter and experience but reason, as form and explanation, because in general discovering what is similar and receiving what is accurate is a peculiar mark of the senses, whereas receiving what is similar and discovering what is accurate is a peculiar mark of reason.

Boethius *De inst. mus.* 5.2 Friedlein 352.4–14

Armonica est facultas differentias acutorum et gravium sonorum
sensu ac ratione perpendens. Sensus enim ac ratio quasi quædam
facultatis armonicæ instrumenta sunt. Sensus namque confusum
quiddam ac proxime tale, quale est illud, quod sentit, advertit.
Ratio vero diiudicat integritatem atque imas persequitur differen-
tias. Itaque sensus invenit quidem confusa ac proxima veritati,
accipit vero ratione integritatem. Ratio vero ipsa quidem in-
venit integritatem, accipit vero confusam ac proximam veri simil-
itudinem. Namque sensus nihil concipit integritatis, sed usque ad
proximum venit, ratio vero diiudicat.

Harmonic science is the faculty of assessing intervals of high-
pitched and low-pitched sounds by means of sense and reason.
For sense and reason are, as it were, particular instruments of
the faculty of harmonic science. For sense observes what it per-
ceives as something confused and very like the sort of thing it
is. But reason judges correctness and pursues basic differences.
Thus, sense in fact discovers things confused and very like the
truth, whereas it receives what is correct from reason. But reason itself in fact discovers correctness and receives a confused
likeness that is very near the truth. For, of course, sense con-
ceives nothing of what is correct but arrives at what is very near
[it]; whereas reason judges [correctness].

When one compares Boethius' version with Ptolemy's original,
it is clear that Boethius is not translating word for word: indeed, as he says of his translation of Nicomachus' *Introductio*
arithmetica, he is following Ptolemy's path, although abridging
and expanding the original as he sees fit. Thus, Boethius' first
two sentences present the definition of harmonic science, omit
the definition of sound[49] and the assertion that sound is the most
general object of hearing, and repeat the claim that reason and
hearing are instruments. But here Boethius goes further than
Ptolemy by adding that reason and hearing are, as it were, instruments of harmonic science. This is odd: there is, after all,
little sense in treating reason as an instrument of harmonic science when this science is a faculty or capacity of reason (or of

the intellect which in one form is reason).[50] Perhaps Boethius has treated κριτήριον μὲν ἀρμονίας (criterion of *harmonia*) as κριτήριον μὲν ἀρμονκῆς (criterion of harmonic science), either because it was written this way in his copy of Ptolemy's text or because he wrongly thought that ἀρμονία is synonymous with ἀρμονική. Or perhaps Boethius was unaware of the philosophical debates about the κριτήριον forming part of the context of Ptolemy's introduction to the *Harmonica*.[51]

At the same time, the qualification, "as it were," suggests that Boethius may already be distancing himself from Ptolemy's view of the instrumentality of reason and hearing in the knowledge of musical intervals, in particular, from the claim that what sense provides is more than the matter of knowledge. At issue for him is whether hearing does under some circumstances lay hold of truth in ascertaining relations among pitches. For, observe that Boethius passes over Ptolemy's argument that reason and hearing are instruments in different ways, that is, as matter and form or as experience and explanation/theory; but presents only the premiss of this argument which he divides into two—(a) that sense apprehends its objects as confused and as like what they really are, whereas reason discerns what is correct (*integritas*) and pursues ultimate distinctions; (b) that sense discovers things confused and like the truth, but must receive correctness from reason, whereas reason itself discovers what is correct and receives from sense a confused likeness that is very near the truth. Though this might seem to be a fair rendering of what Ptolemy has written, Boethius betrays his hand by affirming that reason itself (*ratio ipsa*) discovers what is correct: *ipsa* here has the force of "alone." And were there any doubt, Boethius adds in the final sentence what is nowhere stated in Ptolemy's text, the thesis that sense never apprehends what things really are.

These opening lines from Boethius' translation from the *Harmonica* show the course of what follows. Given that these lines are consistent with Boethius' account in *De inst. mus.* 1.9, one would rightly conclude that Boethius' version concentrates on the sense of what Ptolemy has written and that it is firmly predicated on Boethius' own understanding of what the proper account of harmonic science is. In short, Boethius' translation is interpretative to the point that it makes radical departures from the original. Such departures do not, however, disqualify Boethius' version as a translation: for, if one avoids anachronism by introducing modern notions of accuracy, then it is clear that what Boethius offers here is akin to what he offers in *De institutione arithmetica*, the main difference being that, unlike Nicomachus, Ptolemy holds views profoundly at odds with those Boethius espouses. It remains, then, for us to show that Boethius' departures concern substantive issues in the epistemology and ontology of harmonic science.

Since Boethius has already introduced the thesis that the senses never apprehend the truth about their objects, it is not surprising that he omits Ptolemy's remarks explaining that sensory apprehensions are corrigible by reason, or that he transforms Ptolemy's attempt to clarify this point by means of a simile likening circles drawn by eye or by reason to intervals selected by hearing or in accordance with the proper ratio.[52] For, not only does Boethius suppress Ptolemy's point that the eye can apprehend the difference between the circles, he bypasses the case of hearing entirely.[53] In effect, he abridges the simile to make it illustrate his own thesis about the inability of the sense to lay hold of truth. He then elaborates this by an argument the force of which is that reason corrects and completes error and deficiency in sensation.

This argument draws lightly on the premises, but avoids completely the main point of Ptolemy's own account of the relations of the senses and hearing in harmonic science. In Boethius' view,[54] confusion is attendant upon the senses because they are concerned with matter, and so apprehend forms in matter—forms which are in flux, imperfect, indeterminate, and incomplete (*nec ... atque ad unguem expolitæ*) just as matter is itself—whereas correctness and truth are associated with reason because it is concerned not with matter but with forms studied in separation from their presence in an object (*præter subiecti communionem*). Here, again, Boethius has gone beyond what Ptolemy writes. This time, in adapting Ptolemy's characterization of matter and form in order to support his own epistemological claims about the roles of reason and sense in knowledge, Boethius has introduced a distinction between matter, enmattered form, and form as considered apart from matter. Moreover, on the strength of this, he has concluded that no object of sensation may be accurately perceived as being what it is.[55]

Boethius' treatment of Ptolemy's argument that the senses may apprehend differences correctly when these differences are a large part of what exhibits them proceeds in the same vein: he simply ignores it. As for Ptolemy's claim that the individual sensory apprehensions may contain imperceptible error which accumulates and eventually becomes noticeable, Boethius translates this quite fully since it fits very neatly with his own views;[56] indeed, to ensure that the reader gets the point, Boethius prefaces Ptolemy's example of the division of a line by eye, with his own example of the assessment by hearing of a sequence of consecutive musical intervals. Then, he repeats himself and concludes, "Wherefore no part of judgment[57] should be given to the sense of hearing; but, reason should be brought forth [for this], since it governs and controls erring sense-perception, [and] because sense being fugitive (*labens*) and deficient leans on it as on a cane.[58]

This brings us to the central question of the need for, and the role of, the harmonic *canon*. As one would now expect, Boethius abandons Ptolemy's text at this point. All he says is that this instrument is merely the means by which reason is applied in the study of the correct quantity and measure of interval among sounds. There is no mention *inter alia* of Ptolemy's contention that, when the *canon* is properly set up according to theory and struck, the sound *as heard by most people* is an infallible criterion of truth and falsehood in melodic relations.[59] And the reason for this, we suspect, is that Boethius' conception of harmonic science is radically different from Ptolemy's.

As Ptolemy suggests when discussing the aim of the harmonic theorist, and as he later confirms, the *canon* is not to be used to legislate theory to hearing. Rather, it is the instrument by which hearing and reason interact to reach the truth scientifically understood. Thus, if most people agree on hearing the *canon* that the sound produced according to theory at that time does not seem right, then, apparently, the theory has to be adapted. In most instances, however, the *canon* would presumably disclose little if any disagreement of this sort between what most people hear and the theoretical account of what they hear, though the relation of reason and hearing would still be the same. In Boethius' version, however, the *canon* always legislates to hearing.[60] In other words, if hearing never apprehends musical intervals accurately, audible music is not essentially a cultural phenomenon. It is, instead, the enmattering of intelligible relations which alone are true and precise. These relations are, of course, ratios of whole numbers, and it is these ratios which are, it appears, the object of harmonic science.[61]

The fundamental difference between Ptolemy and Boethius is that for Ptolemy harmonic science is a science essentially of audible sound defined as musical by a community, whereas for Boethius it is a science of purely intelligible numerical relations circumstantially realized in what is heard as well as in what he calls *musica humana* and *musica mundana* in *De inst. mus.* 1.2.

This difference has major consequences when Boethius reports about the rival schools of harmonic science in *De inst. mus.* 5.3. For it is against this background that he first mentions Ptolemy by name in Book 5. According to Boethius, the Pythagoreans (his school) affirm that the aim of harmonic science is to bring all things into agreement with reason: "for it is the role of sense to offer certain seeds of knowledge in some way or other, but it is the role of reason to bring them to fruition."[62] But Aristoxenus (and his followers), in Boethius' view, claim

that "reason is in fact a companion (and a subordinate one) of
sense, that all things are defined by the judgment of sense and
should be held to its regulation (*modulatio*) and agreement." Finally, Boethius continues

> the aim of harmonic science is defined by Ptolemy in another
> way, i.e., that there be nothing antagonistic to the ears and rea-
> son: for, according to Ptolemy, the harmonic theorist apparently
> aims for the result that what the senses point out, reason also
> judges, and that reason discovers ratios only on the condition
> that sense does not object, and that the aim of every harmonic
> theorist should be blended with the concord of these two.[63]

Boethius' representation of Ptolemy's position is, of course, in
error: Ptolemy is cognizant of the variety in acuity and accuracy
of hearing from individual to individual, and he certainly does
not maintain that reason must agree with this sort of standard.
The problem is that Boethius has suppressed all of Ptolemy's
remarks about the third criterion, that is, what most people hear
when the *canon* is set up and struck according to theory. Yet
it is sense defined in this way to which reason or theory must
agree. As for Boethius' version of Ptolemy's criticism of the
Pythagorean and Aristoxenian school, this too loses its force for
the same cause.

Still, one must admit that Boethius has managed Ptolemy very
well. Confronted with an alien account of harmonic science and
its criteria, Boethius has adapted it so that it expresses the sentiments of the Pythagorean school regarding what this science
is about and the use of the *canon*, sentiments underlying the
preceding four books. Then, when he comes to the disputes
between the schools, Boethius mentions Ptolemy and characterizes his views in such a way that it is difficult not to conclude
that Ptolemy is some sort of deviant Pythagorean. Consider the
standpoint of Boethius' Latin reader who has no prior knowledge
of the Greek sources and ask, How else could he view Ptolemy?
Given what Boethius has written in *De inst. mus.* 5.1, and given

how Boethius has characterized reason and sense, each statement in Boethius' report of Ptolemy's account of the goal of
harmonic science has an easy Pythagorean reading. And unless
such a reader could intuit Ptolemy's third criterion and its role in
the very formation of theory, in the phrase, *et ita ratio inveniat,
ut ne sensus reclamat* ("and that reason discovers ratios only on
the condition that sense does not object"),[64] it seems likely that
he would conclude only that Ptolemy is staking out a principle
on the basis of which he can attack the mainstream Pythagorean
analysis of musical intervals.

In sum, Boethius obliterates the motivation for Ptolemy's attack on the rival schools, and, as a consequence, makes him
into a minor Pythagorean who accepts the view that harmonic
science is knowledge of ἁρμονία by means of ratios, and who
disagrees with the majority of his school on a few limited matters in which hearing indicates the possibility of a somewhat
different analysis. It follows, then, that these disagreements are
somewhat arbitrary and have no foundation in theory itself; they
are reduced, in effect, to matters of theoretical taste.[65]

PTOLEMY'S *HARMONICA* AFTER BOETHIUS. One of the questions
about the *fortuna* of Ptolemy's *Harmonica* is, Why was this
treatise on music theory so much less successful in influencing
later theorists than Ptolemy's works on astronomy? The answer,
surely, has little to do with the merit of the *Harmonica* itself.
For it is a sober and sophisticated attempt to establish a science of music that entails some very fundamental criticism of
rival theories. That this book was neglected for so long in the
Latin Middle Ages is, moreover, especially surprising, given that
Ptolemy was recognized as an authority in musical theory and
that the science of music or harmonics was one of a quadrivium
of studies taught in schools as a discipline preparatory to the
study of philosophy and theology.[66] So how, then, is one to explain this lack of attention to a major treatise by a major thinker
in a prominent discipline during the Middle Ages?

Regarding the Latin tradition, we have suggested that, when Ptolemy's *Harmonica* was translated by Boethius from Greek into Latin, it was presented in such a light that is actually seemed to support one of the very schools he criticizes, the Pythagorean. One of the consequences, we suspect, was that Latin readers had little reason thereafter to re-examine the original work in Greek for themselves, a task admittedly made daunting by the technical nature of the subject as well as by Ptolemy's difficult prose style.[67] Yet for want of such a re-reading, Ptolemy's musical theory apparently became in the Latin world a mere variant of the Pythagorean science of music; and so his book, the *Harmonica*, fell into disuse or was not read on its own terms. In a word or two, we submit that Ptolemy's authority was assumed by the heirs of his intellectual opponents in support of their own views and that his departures from majority opinion were comfortably reduced to minor points of dispute about well-circumscribed doctrines. Under such circumstances, it would not be surprising that his book was eclipsed in the shadow of Boethius.

There may have been other reasons as well why Ptolemy's *Harmonica* fell into disuse. But our aim in proposing that one of them might have been how Ptolemy was presented to the Latin world by Boethius, who seems to be his earliest translator, is to emphasize that detailed study of how such translations are actually made may contribute to the understanding of how ideas and documents are transmitted from one culture to another.

BOETHIUS AND EUCLID'S *SECTIO CANONIS*. So far we have considered Boethius' version of a key passage from a source, Ptolemy's *Harmonica*, with which he disagrees fundamentally. Let us now examine how he translates another source, Euclid's *Sectio canonis*, a source that seems, on first glance at least, to be more in line with his own convictions.

The *Sectio canonis* is a brief treatise comprised of an introduction and twenty demonstrations. Unfortunately, the most scholarship has been able to do with it so far is to divide it like Gaul into three parts—the introduction, the first nine demonstrations, and the last eleven—and to attack each by arguing its irrelevance to the others and by denying that Euclid is the author.[68] Though there are some difficult passages in the treatise, the text neither warrants nor supports the sort of interpretation now in play. We have argued elsewhere against this sort of interpretation and in favour of the authenticity, unity, and coherence of the treatise;[69] and we are currently engaged in writing a full study of this text and how it was understood by musical theorists until the modern era. But, for present purposes, we will try to bypass this dispute by concentrating primarily on what we trust are fairly non-controversial, but very interesting, aspects of the relation between the *Sectio canonis* and Boethius' version of it in *De inst. mus.* 4.1–2.[70]

BOETHIUS' VERSION OF EUCLID'S FIRST DEMONSTRATION. Let us begin by comparing the following demonstration from the *Sectio canonis* and its counterpart in the *De institutione musica*.

Euclid *Sectio canonis* prop. 1 Menge 160.6–13

[1] Ἐὰν διάστημα πολλαπλάσιον δὶς συντεθὲν ποιῇ τι διάστημα, καὶ αὐτὸ πολλαπλάσιον ἔσται.

[2] ἔστω διάστημα τὸ ΒΓ, καὶ ἔστω πολλαπλάσιος ὁ Β τοῦ Γ, καὶ γεγενήσθω, ὡς ὁ Γ πρὸς τὸν Β, ὁ Β πρὸς τὸν Δ· [3] φημὶ δὴ τὸν Δ τοῦ Γ πολλαπλάσιον εἶναι. [4] ἐπεὶ γὰρ ὁ Β τοῦ Γ πολλαπλάσιός ἐστι, μετρεῖ ἄρα ὁ Γ τὸν Β. [5] ἦν δὲ καὶ ὡς ὁ Γ πρὸς τὸν Β, ὁ Γ πρὸς τὸν Δ, ὥστε μετρεῖ ὁ Γ καὶ τὸν Δ. [6] πολλαπλάσιος ἄρα ἐστὶν ὁ Δ τοῦ Γ.

[1] If a multiple interval when twice compounded produces an interval, it will itself be multiple as well.
[2] Let *BG* be an interval, and let [the musical note] *B* be a multiple of [the note] *G*, and let *B*:*D* be as *G*:*B*. [3] I say, then, that *D* is a multiple of *G*.
[4] For, since *B* is a multiple of *G*, therefore *G* measures *B*. [5] But, in fact, *B*:*D*[71] was as *G*:*B*, so that *G* also measures *D*. [6] Therefore, [the musical note] *D* is a multiple of *G*.

Boethius *De inst. mus.* 4.2 Friedlein, 302.8–25

[1] *Si intervallum multiplex binario multiplicetur, id quod fit ex hac multiplicatione, intervallum multiplex erit.* [2] *Sit multiplex intervallum*

BC et B multiplex eius, quod est C et fiat, ut est C ad B, ita B ad D.
[3] Quoniam igitur B multiplex est eius, quod est C, metitur C terminus
id, quod est B, vel bis vel tertio vel deinceps. [4] At est ut C ad B ita B
ad D. [5] Metitur igitur B terminus id, quod est D. [6] Quocirca etiam C
terminus id, quod est D, metietur; multiplex est igitur D eius, quod est
C, et est DC intervallum effectum ex composito bis copulatoque sibimet
et per binarium multiplicato BC intervallo. [7] In numeris quoque idem
probatur. [8] Sit enim B ad C duplum, ut binarius ad unitatem et fiat,
ut C ad B ita B ad D. [9] Erit igitur D quaternarius. [10] Multiplex
est autem B ad C id est binarius ad unitatem, multiplex igitur est D
quaternarius ad C unitatem. [11] Est enim quadruplus quaternarius
unitatis et binario multiplicata medietas, quod est intervallum BC.

[1] If a multiple interval is multiplied by 2, what results from this
multiplication will be a multiple interval.
[2] For let *BC* be a multiple interval, that is, [let] *B* [be] a multiple of
C; and let it be that as *C* is to *B* so *B* is to *D*.
[3] Thus, since *B* is a multiple of *C*, the term *C* measures *B* either
twice or three times and so forth. [4] But it is [the case that] as *C* is
to *B* so *B* is to *D*. [5] Thus, the term *B* measures *D*. [6] Wherefore the
term *C* also measures *D*; thus, *D* is a multiple of *C* and the interval *DC*
is produced when the interval *BC* is compounded twice and brought
together with itself, that is, when it is multiplied by 2.
[7] The same [result] is proven also in numbers. [8] For let *B*:*C* be a
duple, like 2:1, and let it be that as *C* is to *B* so *B* is to *D*. [9] Thus,
D will be 4. [10] Now *B*:*C* is multiple, i.e., 2:1; then, (*D* or 4): (*C* or
1) is multiple. [11] For 4:1 is quadruple and a half, the interval *BC*,
multiplied by 2.

The first point to notice is that Boethius' version of Euclid's first
demonstration comes with a second proof ([7]–[11]) which is ab-
sent in the original. Boethius' inclusion of such an extra proof
here—and in five others of the nine demonstrations in the *Sectio canonis* which he translates—is consistent with his remarks
about his mode of translation in the preface to the *De institutione
arithmetica*. Thus, it is possible that Boethius is responsible for
all of them. In any case, the question here is, What is the relation of this alternative proof to the first in Boethius' version? To

answer this, however, one must determine what both his proofs are about.

Boethius' second proof certainly concerns particular numbers. But is his first proof about number in general or magnitude in general? Probably neither. Indeed, it seems to us more likely that both proofs are about musical intervals which are identified as ratios of whole numbers.

Observe that the particular numbers adduced in the second proof define familiar melodic relations, specifically, the octave and double octave. (The same is, in fact, true in the case of all the other demonstrations that have alternative proofs.) Further, consider both of Boethius' proofs and how he writes of *B, C,* for example, and multiplicity. On some occasions, he has *multiplex [est] B eius quod est C* (e.g., [2]). Here, the relation, 'a multiple of,' is presented with one *relatum* as subject and the other as part of the complex predicate (i.e., B is a-multiple-of-C). In effect, the relation is viewed as a property belonging to one *relatum* and specified in terms of the other. But, on other occasions, he writes *multiplex est B ad C* (e.g., [10]). This time, the relation, the ratio *B:C*, is modified by the predicate "multiple." Hence, the relation is at least conceived apart from the *relata* exhibiting it. In Euclid's text there is the analogue of the former locution, πολλαπλάσιος ὁ Β τοῦ Γ (e.g., [2]), but no equivalent of the latter, πολλαπλάσιος ὁ Β πρὸς τὸν Γ, though Euclid does write of ratios when stating proportionalities.[72]

Admittedly, the distinction between talking of *B*'s being related-to-*C* and of the ratio *B:C* is a subtle point in grammar and epistemology. And, granted, these usages, which are common in Greek and Latin technical works, betoken the lack of a developed symbolic notation. For our purposes, however, the occurrence of both in the same proof is yet more evidence that Euclid and Boethius are treating intervals as ratios.[73] For this is, we suspect, what underlies the ease with which Boethius moves from writing of the interval *BC*—a melodic relation defined in terms of its *relata*—to writing of the ratio *B:C*. It is also what justifies his treating *intervalla* as *proportiones* (ratios) in the subsequent demonstrations.[74] Moreover, it serves to explain several other features of the first proof of Boethius' opening demonstration.

For example, in the protasis, where Euclid [1] has διάστημα . . . δὶς συντεθέν (interval . . . twice compounded), Boethius [1] has *binario multiplicetur* (multiplied by two). These are not ordinarily the same. Συντίθεσθαι is a verb for putting things together and, hence, for adding them. *Multiplicare* is a verb for multiplying quanta, that is, for adding them iteratively a certain number of times. Thus, while both verbs signify adding an interval to itself twice, the Latin would suggest that the interval is a quantum and so may be multiplied by a number (viz. scalar multiplication). But clearly, Boethius' *intervallum* is *not* a quantum, since the proof becomes nonsense if an interval is either a magnitude (such as a distance) or a number. Moreover, the proof answers to protasis in either the Greek or Latin version only if an interval is a relation, specifically, if it is a ratio. This is, perhaps, why Boethius explains his use of *multiplicetur*. For in the conclusion to his first proof [6], he writes *intervallum effectum ex composito bis copulatoque sibimet et per binarium multiplicato* (an interval produced by being compounded twice and brought together with itself, that is, when it is multiplied by 2), to show that *multiplicetur* does not signify what is ordinarily called multiplication. Clearly, Boethius is struggling with the technical terminology for manipulating intervals *qua* ratios and is concerned to present clearly to his reader what is meant.

But what are these ratios of? Given that Boethius writes of the interval *BC* and the ratio 2:1, it would seem that the ratios are either of whole numbers or of musical notes. But which? One might think it sufficient to point to some of the later demonstrations in which it would seem that the ratios are of whole numbers.[75] This is the interpretation underlying the current understanding of the first nine demonstrations in the *Sectio canonis*. But, one consequence of this view is that it balkanizes the text by treating these demonstrations as part of "pure" mathematics and, thus, as separate from the last eleven demonstrations which introduce musical notes. So to decide whether this is the whole story, we will have to examine the introduction. Nevertheless, the text of Euclid's first demonstration confirms that these are indeed the proper choices, because of the masculine singular definite article that attaches to each letter: the *B*, for instance, in the first proof is either an ἀριθμός or a φθόγγος. Granted, Boethius uses *terminus* in his version, and so appears to suppose that the word understood (though not stated by Euclid) is ὅρος (term). But this is a minor point of no real significance, since Boethius does follow Euclid in understanding what the ratios are ratios of.

BOETHIUS' VERSION OF THE INTRODUCTION TO THE *SECTIO CANONIS*. Comparison of the introduction to Euclid's *Sectio canonis* with Boethius' translation shows that the broad outlines of the argument in the two documents are similar. Both begin by elaborating deductively the conditions for the occurrence of (musical) sound. Next, both explain the relation between these conditions and the pitch of (musical) sound. Finally, their respective analyses of the nature and causes of the variation of pitch become the basis for inferences to the effect that relations among musical sounds *qua* pitches are to be defined by ratios of whole numbers.[76] At this point, however, the two treatises diverge. Euclid argues for a special relation between concordant sounds and multiple and superparticular ratios; whereas Boethius connects these two sorts of ratio with discords as well as concords and concludes by stating Euclid's characterizations of concordance and discordance.[77]

Apart from this broad similarity between Boethius' version of the introduction to the *Sectio canonis* and the original, it appears that Boethius has been quite creative in adapting his source. Some of his divergences in terminology and mode of expression are important enough to merit attention in a fuller account of his rendering of the *Sectio canonis*. For now, however, we will concentrate on one fundamental point at which Boethius recasts the Euclidean conceptual framework. The sentence in question is,

Sed omnis motus habet in se tum velocitatem tum etiam tarditatem.

But, every motion has in itself both speed and slowness.

The first thing to settle about this sentence is that *tum . . . tum etiam* does not signify, as Bower would have it,[78] that every motion is at one time fast and at another time slow. Boethius' contention is not that a single motion produces changes in pitch over time by virtue of the change in its speed. Rather, as the collocation of these particles suggests,[79] he is proposing that each motion is faster than some but slower than others—which would be consistent with what Euclid writes.[80] Thus, the sound this motion produces is understood as having *relative* pitch. The question is, Why does Boethius present the relevant *differentia* of motions as relative speed, when in the original it is relative πυκνότης or numerosity of motion.[81] This is especially puzzling, since, in *De inst. mus.* 1.3, Boethius actually uses forms of the proper Latin equivalents of ἀραιότεραι and πυκνότεραι in describing motions, *rariores* and *spissiores*, when he says:

Sed quoniam iunctæ sunt velocitates sonorum, nulla intercapedo sentitur auribus et unus sonus sensum pellit vel gravis vel acutus, quamvis uterque ex pluribus constet gravis quidem ex tardioribus et rarioribus acutus vero ex celeribus ac spissis.

But, since the rapid motions of sounds are joined together, no interruption is heard by the ears and one sound, either low or high in pitch, strikes hearing, although each is comprised of many sounds—low-pitched [sound] in fact by slower [motions] that are less close together and high-pitched [sounds] by motions that are faster and close together.[82]

The issue here is how numerical analysis is relevant to the phenomenon of pitch, an analysis which lies at the very heart of the theory Euclid and Boethius are expounding. To Boethius, the critical feature of sound is its pitch, and variations of pitch are due to variations in the speed of the motions producing the sounds. But Euclid holds that the critical feature is not the speed of the motions but their number or compactness. In sum, whereas

Boethius proposes to quantify the pitch of two sounds by quantifying the relative speeds of the motions producing them, Euclid seeks to quantify the pitch of two sounds by determining the relative number of the motions effecting the sounds. Indeed, Euclid is prepared simply to say that the sounds are composed of motions,[83] thereby reducing sound to number. To avoid this particular reduction, Boethius construes Euclid's claim as an explanation of the phenomenal datum that the sound we hear is not many but one, thus leaving intact his own thesis that the pitch of a sound depends on the speed of the motion producing the sound. This is, we think, what underlies the qualifying, "as it were" (*quasi*),[84] which Boethius inserts into

Unde fit, ut omnis sonus quasi ex quibusdam partibus compositus esse videatur

Whence it results that every musical sound seems to be composed, as it were, from certain parts

when he translates Euclid's conclusion,

διόπερ ἐκ μορίων τοὺς φθόγγους συγκεῖσθαι φατέον, ἐπειδὴ προσθέσει καὶ ἀφαιρέσει τυγχάνουσι τοῦ δέοντος

Wherefore, we should say that musical notes are composed of parts, since they reach what is needed by addition and subtraction.

We now return to our question about the ratios in the first demonstration. According to Boethius, ratios of whole numbers hold between the pitches of musical sounds and are (presumably) to be quantified in terms of the speeds of the motions that produce the sounds;[85] whereas for Euclid, these whole-number ratios obtain between sounds because the sounds are composed of discrete motions. Now we come to the tension in the introductions and demonstrations offered by both authors between saying that the ratios *quantify* relations among musical sounds and saying that these relations are *really* just ratios of whole numbers. This tension in either text is the result of an ontological reduction: both authors treat ratios not only as explanatory principles for quantifying relations among pitches, but also as what the pitch-relations really are.

This, then, explains why the demonstrations in the *Sectio canonis* and in the *De institutione musica* may refer to ratios of whole numbers and still be limited in scope to relations between musical notes. Moreover, in light of our previous remarks about treating relations either as properties of *relata* or as independent of them, it also becomes clear that this ontological reduction explains why both authors, in treating intervals as ratios, often write of the interval *BC* and the ratio *B:C*, as though pairs of musical sounds were in reality pairs of whole numbers. In particular, it explains the relevance of Boethius' illustrative use of the numbers that define basic melodic intervals/ratios in his alternative proofs. Accordingly, this ontological reduction which Euclid makes and Boethius accepts, though he views it differently, is the key to the unity of the *Sectio canonis* as a whole and its Latin translation.[86] More specifically, given that this ontological reduction of intervals to ratios is peculiar to the analysis of musical relations and that there is no evidence (so far as we are aware) of the sort of argument about intervals *qua* whole-number ratios found in the *Sectio canonis* outside a musical context, it follows, first, that the introduction is for Euclid and Boethius essential to understanding the demonstrations and, second, that the first demonstration does not, as is usually maintained, set out to prove some 'abstract' truth about whole-number ratios in general.[87]

Unfortunately, we must leave the matter here. Pursuing it further now would take us too deeply into the argument and language of Euclid's *Sectio canonis* and of Boethius' translation. Our primary interest here is in Boethius' role as a translator and we have already uncovered enough to get a sense of his treatment of Euclid's treatise.

It should by clear that when Boethius departs from Euclid's original by introducing the idea of the relative speed of the motions producing sound, he is not, in our view, guilty of careless translation. His divergence from Euclid's text marks a substantial difference in basic doctrine, and only by departing from Euclid can Boethius maintain the consistency of his analysis in the *De institutione musica* and, specifically, introduce Book 4 as a recapitulation of what precedes.[88] As for the question of whether Boethius actually made this change or whether, as Bower suggests,[89] he is instead translating (accurately) from a source in which the change had already been made, the former alternative is preferable, especially since there is no external evidence for the latter.

How one estimates the significance of Boethius' departures from the *Sectio canonis* will be influenced by one's view of the much repeated claim that the *Sectio canonis* is a Pythagorean document.[90] Granted, Boethius follows the Pythagoreans and he does appropriate what Euclid has written; but this does not make the *Sectio canonis* Pythagorean. After all, as we have shown, Boethius does the same to Ptolemy's *Harmonica*, and this treatise is undeniably opposed to the Pythagorean school of thought about the science of music. That Euclid's rationale for analyzing sounds by means of the ratios of whole numbers is different from Boethius' is clear. Equally clear is the fact that Euclid's rationale is also at odds with the one offered, according to Porphyry, by Archytas of Tarentum, a Pythagorean of the early fourth century BC, a rationale which is pretty much the one Boethius presents. Indeed, one might be tempted to argue on the strength of this that the *Sectio canonis* is not Pythagorean at all.[91] Still, the assumption that it is or that Euclid was an adherent of some amalgam of Platonism and Pythagoreanism in the late fourth century BC is well entrenched. Let us, therefore, examine this assumption briefly.

EUCLID AND PYTHAGOREANISM. The question of Euclid's philosophical allegiances has been debated since ancient times. The truth of the matter is that there is no good evidence that Euclid subscribed to any school of thought, and those inferences that he was a Platonist or a Pythagorean which are based on some estimation of the character of the treatises that have come to us under his name, are poor indeed.[92] It seems, in fact, that one of the unspoken grounds for such claims is the belief that Euclid flourished around 300 BC. Hence, it goes, he must have been familiar with the first generation of Platonist and Aristotelians, and even party to their views. But Euclid's dates are uncertain and, were one to assign him a floruit, 300 BC would likely be too early.

It is customary to rely on an anecdote told by Proclus (410–485)[93] in which Euclid advises Ptolemy Soter (who reigned from 304 to 282 BC) that there is no royal road to geometry, and to interpret this anecdote to mean that Euclid actually lived during the time of Soter and so flourished *ca.* 300 BC. It is also customary to follow Proclus in drawing support for this conclusion from Archimedes' (*ca.* 287 to 212 BC) (trivial) citation of Euclid in *De sphæra et cylindro* 1. prop. 2 and of a work entitled *Elements* in prop. 6. But this is all very weak. The same anecdote is told of Menaechmus, a geometer of the fourth century BC, and Alexander the Great (356–323 BC), in Stobaeus, *Eclogæ physicæ et ethicæ* 2.31.115; and so it has no credibility of its own. Moreover, the purported citation of Euclid by Archimedes may be in fact an early interpolation; and the reference to the *Elements* need not be to Euclid's *Elements*.[94] Thus, at the most, all one may glean from this is that Euclid was either a predecessor or a contemporary of Archimedes.

If, however, Euclid is the author of the *Phænomena*, then it is possible to argue on the strength of linguistic and conceptual evidence, in particular, his use of the traditional names for the zodiacal signs (or twelfths of the zodiacal circle), that Euclid lived in the last half of the third century.[95] Admittedly, it is not certain that Euclid wrote the *Phænomena*. As Menge reports,[96] Theodosius of Bithynia (first century BC) is the first to mention a book entitled *Phænomena*—though, as Menge points out, ὡς ἐν τοῖς φαινομένοις δέδεικται (as is proven in the *Phænomena*) may be an interpolation—and Galen (129–195) is the first to say that Euclid is its author. But, though Pappus (late third and early fourth centuries AD) as well as Marinus and Philoponus (both active in the 6th century AD) also speak of a *Phænomena* by Euclid, the *Phænomena* is not listed as one of Euclid's works by Proclus at *In Euc.* prol. 2 (Friedlein 69.1–4)—however, neither are Euclid's *Porismata* and the *Data*, for that matter. On balance, then, it seems that there are no decisive arguments for doubting that Euclid was the author of this handbook of spherical astronomy. And, so, it is possible that his main intellectual activity belongs to the latter part of the third century BC.[97]

In any event, it is impossible to infer the nature of Euclid's aims in writing the *Sectio canonis* on the basis of a theory about his date and some fuzzy notion of what his projects must have been, given such a date. Moreover, the fact that this treatise is abridged by Boethius so that it fits seamlessly into his version of the Pythagorean school likewise does not license the inference that Euclid was expressing the views of a Pythagorean sect in this treatise. Nor does the fact that the *Sectio canonis* overlaps in some of its doctrines with those expressed in earlier documents known to be Pythagorean warrant downplaying the points where it does not overlap, and concluding, again, that it is a Pythagorean text.

In truth, to appreciate the significance of what Boethius has done to Euclid's treatise in translating it, one must abandon the superficial categories used by modern scholars to characterize intellectual allegiances and turn instead to the question of how the ancients viewed themselves and depicted their opponents, by diligently distinguishing on the basis of documentary evidence what counts for them as a Pythagorean in the various periods of antiquity. Such a regimen will uncover two data: that Euclid's intellectual allegiances are not determinable and that Boethius' allegiances, though still the matter of scholarly debate, were of the sort to permit his following doctrine which he calls Pythagorean in his works on *arithmetica* and harmonic science.

CONCLUSION. In the preceding remarks, we have made a case *prima facie* that Boethius' translation of the *Sectio canonis* and the *Harmonica* from Greek into Latin is a subtle adaptation of these works to an alien project, the exposition of what in his time was recognized as a Pythagorean science of music. To develop our case further, it would be necessary to examine the Greek sources and to determine in greater detail their representation in the *De institutione musica*. At the same time, it would also be necessary to determine what Boethius' Pythagorean science of music is by examining not only the *De institutione musica* but also those other works by Boethius in which he discusses science, its objects, and its means for obtaining knowledge. In other words, to understand how Boethius has adapted his Greek sources through translation in order to present his own views, one must eventually understand both his sources and his views.

More generally, we suggest that today one does not gain insight into a document such as *De institutione musica* by applying the customary philological methods and assumptions of modern scholarship. For example, one does not understand such documents simply by identifying their Greek and Latin sources: though this is not always a necessary first step, by itself it merely presumes to fragment such documents into unrelated pieces. Nor does one come closer to grasping what the *De institutione musica* and other texts like it are about by arguing that they contain bad translations of their sources now extant, or that they are good translations of variants of these sources no longer extant. In both cases, the error lies in the application of modern and inappropriate criteria of accuracy. To reach satisfactory interpretations of documents containing translations, or even quotations, of other works, one must ask whether the authors, in offering such excerpts, have adapted the originals to indicate and support their own views and whether their doing so is in accordance with the standards of translation and quotation they announce or in force at their time.

In conclusion, we return to our distinction of modern and pre-modern translations. Throughout the preceding study of Boethius' translations of Euclid's *Sectio canonis* and Ptolemy's *Harmonica*, we have insisted that it is inappropriate to assess them using modern criteria of accuracy as a yard-stick. Our reason for this is that when Boethius' translations are viewed in this light, one trivializes the "inaccuracies" and misses their importance as signs of how he adapts these texts to his own conceptual framework and purposes. It is possible, however, to take Boethius' remarks about translation and to restate the matter in such a way that the gulf between the modern translator and Boethius is clearer.

Suppose that both are concerned with accuracy. But accuracy regarding what? The words or the sense? If one grants that Boethius was determined to render the sense of his sources, then the sense he renders is his own understanding of what they were really trying to say: it is not their understanding of what they wrote. Thus, Boethius' version of the treatises by Euclid and Ptolemy is interpretative because it is contingent on his own views—indeed, as we have shown, it is highly interpretative because the words they actually wrote do not serve as a significant constraint. Thus, Boethius is unlike his modern counterpart. Nowadays, the dichotomy of words and sense is not likely to be accepted, since it is in the final analysis false. Translators today are stricter about what counts as a suitable representation of an author's meaning: the meaning they seek to represent is less obviously determined by considerations alien to the text and is expected to be verifiable by recourse to the original documents themselves. What lies behind this contrast is not only a reluctance to accept a choice between translating words and translating sense, but also the deeper fact that the modern notion and practice of intellectual history, that is, of reporting the ideas of others, is quite different from the ancient.[98] Still, like

Boethius, modern translators do interpret their sources and their interpretations have a rhetorical context. After all, consider the differences between the numerous English translations of the *Bible* or of Plato's *Republic* during the last century, for instance. Clearly, even within the guidelines of a need for accuracy and some sort of verifiability, modern translators find ample room for significant disagreement. And these disagreements have to be understood in terms of the aims and beliefs of the various translators and their intended readers.

Thus, however one analyzes the differences between a modern translator and a pre-modern translator such as Boethius, it remains true that translators are always interpreters, and that a translation may displace, but never replace, the work translated. Moreover, it would seem to be a corollary that, when the original is lost, no translation is by itself a basis for recovering it.

NOTES

We are grateful to Bernard R. Goldstein, W. R. Knorr, and M.R. Maniates for their comments on an earlier draft of this paper.

1. See L. Minio-Paluello "Boethius" *Dictionary of Scientific Biography [DSB]* ed. C. C. Gillispie (New York 1970–80) 228–30, 230–5; A. H. Armstrong ed. *The Cambridge History of Later Greek and Early Medieval Philosophy* (Cambridge 1970) 539.

2. *Arithmetica* is not what we call arithmetic; it is, rather, a philosophical theory of number itself that is opposed traditionally to the computational theory of numbered things and allied with arithmology or number-magic. Its roots lie in early Pythagoreanism and its development was fostered by the Hellenistic tradition of Platonic commentary. See M. L. D'Ooge trans. *Nicomachus of Gerasa: Introduction to Arithmetic* (London 1926) 16–34.

3. The two treatises on geometry which have come down to us under Boethius' name are now thought to be spurious, though based perhaps on Boethius' work; and if Boethius actually wrote a treatise on astronomy, it has apparently been lost. See Minio-Paluello "Boethius" 230–1, 233.

4. G. Friedlein ed. *Anicii Manlii Torquati Severini Boetii De institutione arithmetica libri duo, De institutione musica libri quinque* (Leipzig 1867) 4.27–5.4.

5. See F. Rosenthal *The Classical Heritage in Islam* trans. E. and J. Marmorstein (Berkeley and Los Angeles 1975) 17–9.

6. Bower's paraphrase and quotation of this passage, in "Boethius and Nicomachus: An Essay Concerning the Sources of the *De institutione musica*" *Vivarium* 1 (1978) 2–3, overlooks the conjunctive particle *non*, and his later translation, *Fundamentals of Music* (New Haven and London 1989) xxv, appears to misread the syntax: *at* (but, whereas, yet) introduces the entire sentence up to *constringo* (I confine), and *sed* (but) immediately after this verb should not be ignored. (Bower's policy of omitting Latin particles is sometimes the cause of error: Boethius' connectives, resumptives, and adversatives are nowhere near as pointless as Bower supposes.) Moreover, given its position, it seems unlikely that *non* in *at non alterius obnoxius* is adherescent with *obnoxius*: in fact, it is somewhat emphatic and so one might translate it "but it is not the case that I. . . ." In short, Boethius' point is not that he actually follows the strictest (Bower's "rather strict" misses the superlative) rule of translation though not as a slave (there is no such negative concession in the text); rather, Boethius is saying that he does not follow the strictest rule at all. For he abridges and supplements the original. M. Masi's version actually approaches the sense here: *Boethian Number Theory: A Translation of the* De Institutione Arithmetica (Amsterdam 1983), 67. For a critical review of Masi, see A. C. Bowen's review *Ancient Philosophy* 9 (1989) 137–43.

7. Regarding the latter science, this follows from the general character of the *De inst. mus.*, in particular, the references and treatment of Pythagoras and the Pythagoreans, and how claims Boethius makes in his own voice (usually first person plural) compare with views he attributes to the Pythagoreans. See *De inst. mus.* 1.9 (see *n*62), 2.21–7, 5.8. As for *arithmetica*, this follows from the fact that Nicomachus' *Introductio arithmetica*, the text that Boethius translates, is unmistakably a work presented in the Pythagorean school.

8. "Boethius and Nicomachus," *Fundamentals of Music* xiv–xix; see also J. Solomon "A Preliminary Analysis of the Organization of Ptolemy's *Harmonics*" *Music Theory and its Sources: Antiquity and the Middle Ages* ed. A. Barbera (Notre Dame 1990) 69.

9. Minio-Paluello "Boethius" 230.

10. "Ptolemy" *DSB* 187.

11. K. von Jan ed. *Musici scriptores graeci* (Leipzig 1895) 275.7. Bower, in "Boethius and Nicomachus" 8*n*20, seems to think that the excerpts were taken from another work by Nicomachus which is no longer extant, because *Harm. man.* 1, 12 promise a more detailed introduction to harmonic science in several books. But such promises need not mean that the introduction in question was ever written. Moreover, the relation of this compilation to Nicomachus' *Harm. man.* is more complex than Bower allows. In our opinion, a careful reading indicates that many of the so-called excerpts are culled from, or report views in, texts other than the *Harm. man.* Whether these texts were also by Nicomachus is a nice question that invites speculation, but lacks the means of confirmation.

12. According to Porphyry, the bulk of the *Harmonica* comes from Didymus, a musician and theorist of the first century AD. See *Porphyrios Kommentar zur Harmonielehre des Klaudios Ptolemaios* ed. I. Düring *Göteborg Högskolas Årsskrift* 38 (Göteborg 1932) 5.11–16. Since Didymus' writings have not been preserved except in reports, the claim that he is the source of the *Harmonica* cannot be confirmed. There is a real possibility, however, that the claim is polemical (see *Porphyrios Kommentar* 29.27–33). Porphyry's main criticism that Ptolemy (*Harm.* 1.3) wrongly supposes the distinction of high and low notes to be one of quantity (ποσότης) rather than one of quality (ποιότης) is fundamental.

13. *Commentarii in somnium Scipionis* 1.19–26 *Macrobius* ed. J. Willis 2 vols (Leipzig 1970).

14. For a critical account of the scholarly effort to determine Macrobius' sources, see W. H. Stahl *Macrobius: Commentary on the Dream of Scipio* (New York and London 1952) 23–9.

15. We will overlook for now the debate about the relation between *De inst. mus.* 4.18 and *Harm.* 1.8; see Bower *Fundamentals of Music* 161*n*93, 181–3, xxxv–vi.

16. Minio-Paluello, in "Boethius" 229, speculates that Marius Victorinus (fourth century AD), the author of a Latin adaptation of Porphyry's *Introductio* used by Boethius, may have encouraged Boethius to present as original work what he was in fact adapting from the Greek.

17. See Bower "Boethius and Nicomachus" 43, *Fundamentals of Music* 162*n*1.

18. The following remarks on *Harm.* 1.1–2 have profited from A. A. Long's valuable discussion of Ptolemy's *De iudicandi facultate.* Long maintains that the epistemology set out in this treatise is, in fact, intended to justify what one finds in Ptolemy's scientific works such as *Harmonica;* see "Ptolemy *On the Criterion:* An Epistemology for the Practicing Scientist" *The Question of "Eclecticism"* edd. J. M. Dillon and A. A. Long (Berkeley and Los Angeles 1988) 193–6, 202–4. For another account of these chapters which emphasizes matters of their form and its numerological significance, see Solomon "A Preliminary Analysis" with *n*22.

19. *De iud. fac.* 1.1; Long "Ptolemy *On the Criterion*" 180. In accordance with Ptolemy's usage in *De iud. fac.* 1.1–4.1 and *Harm.* 1.1–2, and his decision to ignore the techinical vocabulary current among philosophers of his time in favor of a simpler vocabulary that suffices to aid non-experts and to clarify reflection on the realities signified (*De iud. fac.* 4.2–6.3), the term "criterion"—which is to render the Greek word, κριτήριον—is to be understood to encompass (a) the object about which one makes judgments, (b) the means through which and the means by which judgments about such objects are made, (c) the agent of judgment, (d) the goal of the judgments made, as well as the more usual sense, (e) the standard(s) by which the truth of judgment is assessed. See H. Blumenthal "Plotinius and Proclus on the Criterion of Truth" *The Criterion of Truth: Essays in Honour of George Kerferd* edd. P. Huby and G. Neal (Liverpool 1989) 257–8. Note that in his general account of the criterion, Ptolemy (*De iud. fac.* 1.1: cf. 2.1) writes of a criterion of what there is (τῶν ὄντων) and not of a criterion for truth. For him, truth is a criterion *qua* goal of judgment (cf. *De iud. fac.* 2.1–2).

20. Long "Ptolemy *On the Criterion*" 192.

21. The passage in question is difficult, so in what follows we will keep to the text very closely in order to develop our interpretation. For a useful translation of the *Harmonica,* see Barker *Greek Musical Writings;* II. Harmonic and Acoustic Theory (Cambridge and New York 1989).

22. *Harm.* ed. I. Düring *Die Harmonielehre des Klaudios Ptolemaios Göteborg Högskolas Årsskrift* 36 (Göteborg 1930) 3.1–4. Solomon objects to such a rendering on the grounds that if harmonics is a science, it cannot be a capacity. See "A Preliminary Analysis" 71. But the claim that any science is a capacity is plausible *prima facie*: after

all, to acquire scientific knowledge is to acquire an ability. In any case, such claims were articulated and analysed by Plato and Aristotle and are familiar throughout the history of ancient thought as well as today. Moreover, Solomon's alternative, "Harmonics is a perceptive function of the differences in sounds between high and low," is difficult to understand; and the main premiss he offers in defence of it (that hearing what is audible offers the ability to hear sounds) is mistaken.

Solomon's further contention (p. 72) that the Greek text translated is comprised of fifteen words—which he takes to be significant because there are the same number of notes in the double octave—ignores the evidence of certain manuscripts that Ptolemy wrote sixteen words. As for the next eleven words defining sound and affirming that sound is the first and most general thing heard—see *De iud. fac.* 11.1 for the claim that sound is the proper object of hearing—Solomon remarks that this makes a total of twenty-eight words, the same number as there are notes in Lesser Perfect System, without pausing to mention the possibility that these words were originally a marginal comment which some copyist has included in the text. See also pp. 81–2, in which he develops this numerological assessment and concludes that it reveals Ptolemy's "inchoate concern for some organization dependent on the tetraktys."

Two points should be made about this sort of speculation. First, even were it true, it does not seem to bear on the meaning of what Ptolemy actually writes; and it is this meaning that ultimately determines the organization of the *Harmonica*. Second, Solomon's attempts to support his "discovery" of Ptolemy's interest in the Pythagorean τετρακτύς by reference to the organization of other treatises are misguided: the division of Greek texts into books, chapters, and so on, is often the contribution of mediaeval copyists and editors. Thus, citing the divisions in the manuscript tradition and in the critical editions based on it (cf. p. 70*n*14) proves nothing: the only credible evidence for how the documents were originally articulated must be gleaned from internal references and from citations in works of the same period. For example, in the case of Ptolemy's *Almagest*, which Solomon cites, G. J. Toomer concludes that it was originally divided only into books, that the division into chapters and the related headings as well as the table of contents are spurious. See Toomer *Ptolemy's Almagest* (New York and Berlin 1984) 5.

23.   Hearing and reason are both instrumental, though the mode of their instrumentality differs, as Ptolemy's use of different instrumental constructions at *De iud. fac.* 1.5, 2.3–4 indicates: hearing, like any other sense, is "the means through which" (τὸ δι' οὗ) one make judgments and reason is "the means by which" (τὸ ᾧ) one does this. Note that one of the basic meanings of κριτήριον is "instrument." Long's claim ("Ptolemy *On the Criterion*" 189–90, 196) that in the *De iudicandi facultate* Ptolemy does not make reason a criterial instrument has the difficulty that ᾧ in the phrase ᾧ κρίνει, is an instrumental dative, and the Ptolemy himself likens both reason and sense-perception to instruments (ὄργανα) at *De iud. fac.* 2.3: cf. *De inst. mus.* Friedlein 352.5–6. See also Long "Ptolemy *On the Criterion*" 197: "On Ptolemy's scheme, intellect uses *logos*. . . ."

24.   *Harm.* ed. I. Düring 3.3–5: καὶ κριτήρια μὲν ἁρμονίας ἀκοὴ καὶ λόγος, οὐ κατὰ τὸν αὐτὸν δὲ τρόπον, ἀλλ᾽ ἡ μὲν ἀκοὴ παρὰ τὴν ὕλην καὶ τὸ πάθος, ὁ δὲ λόγος παρὰ τὸ εἶδος καὶ τὸ αἴτιον. Barker's translation of these lines, in *Greek Musical Writings* 276, seems to misconstrue them: the phrases introduced by παρὰ probably answer to κατὰ . . . τρόπον. Long misstates Ptolemy's point by taking ἀκοή to signify sound. See "Ptolemy *On the Criterion*" 202. As for the analogy itself, matter is presumably to be taken in relation to form and πάθος in relation to explanation: so rather than Barker's rendering of πάθος by "modification," which is a synonym for change or enmattered form, we suggest "experience," since this is what the senses report to reason: see Ptolemy, *De iud. fac.* 8.3, 10.1–3; Barker *Greek Musical Writings* 280*n*20.

25.   *Harm.* Düring 3.5–8, 8–12.

26.   See *Harm.* Düring 3.13: ἐπί γε τῶν δι' αἰσθήσεως νοητῶν. Barker, in *Greek Musical Writings* 276, has "at least in the case of things that can be detected through sensation." Ptolemy may here be thinking that there are things known by reason without the aid of the senses, a thesis he accepts in his *De iud. fac.* 10.5.

27.   *Harm.* Düring 3.12,14, 14–17.

28.   *Harm.* Düring 3.17–20. See also *De iud. fac.* 8.3–5, 9.6.

29.   *Harm.* Düring 3.20–4.7, 4.7–13, 4.13–5.2.

30.   *Harm.* Düring 3.20–4.7.

31.   *Greek Musical Writings* 277*n*9. See also *De iud. fac.* 8.3–5, 10.1–3.

32. In *De iud. fac.* 10.4–5 Ptolemy also writes that on certain occasions reason may choose to correct sense-perception through the means of sense-perceptions. Specifically, he maintains that, if a sense is affected in a way inappropriate to the object sensed, reason may either determine the error through similar, unaffected or uncorrupted sense-perceptions when the cause of error involves the sense-perceptions, or it may do this through dissimilar sense-perceptions of the same object when the cause does not involve them but something external.

33. For a different reading of the role of this premiss in Ptolemy's argument, see Barker *Greek Musical Writings* 277n9. Barker's translation on p. 276 modifies the syntax of Düring's text, *Harm.* 4.7–13. Solomon's version of these lines goes astray ("A Preliminary Analysis" 73–4), and this vitiates his account of what follows: (a) πρὸς αὐτάς does not mean "in these areas"—the antecedent of αὐτάς is αἰσθήσεων; (b) and "at least those found in the greater parts" misconstrues τὰς γοῦν μείζοσι ἐν μέρεσιν ὧν εἰσι λαμβανομένας. See Barker *Greek Musical Writings* 277.

34. This is made clear in the text lines, when Ptolemy considers the conditions under which imperceptible error in sense-perception may accumulate and eventually become perceptible.

35. *De iud. fac.* 10.1–3, in which Ptolemy affirms that the senses are infallible in so far as they only report their impressions or affections, and states that sense-perception sometimes reports falsely about the objects perceived—which suggests that sometimes it may report the truth: cf. *De iud. fac.* 10.6, and 11.1 where hearing is said to be capable of making true reports about its proper object.

36. *De iud. fac.* 12.4. Long's claim, in "Ptolemy *On the Criterion*" 193, that, for Ptolemy, ". . . sense-perception is limited to the immediate experiences it undergoes and it cannot pass any judgment on any external object as such," though it neglects καὶ ἐπὶ ποσὸν ἀπαλλαγέντων at *De iud. fac.* 8.5, does draw attention to one of a number of puzzles in the *De iudicandi facultate*: for, though Ptolemy does say at *De iud. fac.* 8.4 that sense-perception simply judges only its affections and not their objects, his remarks at 10.2–3 and 11.1 suggest that he also holds that the senses report truly (ἀληθεύειν) or falsely (ψεύδεσθαι) about their objects (cf. *De iud. fac.* 12.6). Perhaps, he is assuming some distinction between judging (κρίνειν) these objects and reporting truly or falsely about them. In any case, that sense-perception

is capable of the veridical apprehension of objects is a key premiss in the argument of the *Harmonica*.

37. *Harm*. Düring 4.13–5.2.

38. In *De iud. fac.* 2.4–5, Ptolemy distinguishes φαντασία (*phantasia*), which is the impression and transmission to the intellect of information reached by contact through the sense organs, and ἔννοια (conception), which is the possession and retention of these transmissions in memory. Thus, the conceptions are what may become scientific if suitably integrated into theory.

39. *Harm*. Düring 5.2–10.

40. *Harm*. Düring 5.11–13, 13–19.

41. Euclid introduces a monochord (κανών) in the last two demonstrations of the *Sectio canonis*, H. Menge ed. *Euclidis phænomena et scripta musica* 178.12–180.31 **Euclidis opera omnia** 7 ed. J. L. Heiberg (Leipzig 1916), and Boethius assumes a monochord in Books 1–4 of *De inst. mus.* See Friedlein 351.15–7. Ptolemy calls such a monochord the harmonic *canon* (*Harm*. Düring 66.6–15). He explains its use in *Harm.* 1.8, criticizes it in *Harm.* 2.12, and then outlines ways in which it may be improved in *Harm.* 2.13. Ptolemy (*Harm.* 1.11) also describes the use of an eight-string *canon* to demonstrate that the octave is less than six tones, as well as a fifteen-string *canon* to display the double octave system (*Harm.* 3.1).

42. In the *Almagest*, Ptolemy uses ὑποθέσεις in reference to his planetary models. See Toomer *Ptolemy's Almagest* 23–4. We have adopted this usage here because the ensuing contrast of arithmetical and geometrical models highlights the relation between harmonic science and astronomy.

43. Barker's note on this passage (*Greek Musical Writings* 278n15) is too sweeping in its generalization of a distinction between phenomena and "objective reality:" in effect, Barker gives too little credence to Ptolemy's third criterion, a criterion which entails that the true state of affairs is under certain circumstances fully perceptible. Further, we do not agree with Barker that the theoretician's ὑποθέσεις are externally existent principles underlying and supporting the phenomena.

Ptolemy continues by adding that the harmonic theorist and the astronomer are obliged to maintain their respective ὑποθέσεις because in everything it is characteristic of the theoretician and scientist "to demonstrate that the works of nature are crafted with a particular reason and with a fixed cause and that nothing is produced by nature at

random and circumstantially, especially in its most beautiful constructions, the sort of thing that the more rational senses, hearing and vision,
are." See *Harm.* Düring 5.19–24. Barker translates ὁποῖαι τυγχάνουσιν
αἱ τῶν λογικωτέρων αἰσθήσεων, ὄψεως καὶ ἀκοῆς by "the kinds [*scil.*
constructions] that belong to the more rational of the senses, sight and
hearing." See *Greek Musical Writings* 279. The syntax allows either
reading: τῶν λογικωτέρων αἰσθήσεων is construed as partitive in the
former and as possessive in the latter. The question is whether this
clause affirms the reliability of the senses of hearing and sight or the
intelligibility of the objects of these senses. Our version is, perhaps,
more in keeping with Ptolemy's concern with the third criterion.

44. See Long "Ptolemy *On the Criterion*" 189. In our view,
the claim made by Blumenthal, Long, *et alii* ("*On the Kriterion and
Hegemonikon:* Claudius Ptolemæus" *The Criterion of Truth* 217) that
Ptolemy nowhere uses κριτήριον to signify a standard is mistaken.

45. See *Harm.* Düring 3.17–21.

46. *Harm.* Düring 5.16–19. In this respect, then, the *Harm.* extends the account of sense-perception found in the *De iud. fac.* and of its
relation to reason. Though both treatises acknowledge that the senses
may on occasion report truly about the objects sensed and, thus, that
there be true opinions about these objects, the former makes a well-
defined subset of these true opinions essential to one exact science,
harmonics, by making them serve as a standard for the development
and confirmation of theory. This is, in our view, consistent with what
Ptolemy writes in the *De iud. fac.*, and so we do not follow Long in
inferring that the *De iud. fac.* presents science as "a stable and incon-
trovertible state of the intellect, consisting in self-evident and expert
discrimination." See "Ptolemy *On the Criterion*" 194.

At *De iud. fac.* 3.2, Ptolemy likens opinion (δόξα) and knowledge
(ἐπιστήμη) to a legal decision or judgment that is "unclear somehow
and suspect, against which someone might indeed appeal" and to one
that is "very clear and accepted," respectively. In the present context,
one might take this to mean that proper theory does not itself come
into conflict with the apprehensions of the majority about the sizes of
the intervals they hear when the *canon* is correctly set up and struck,
that such conflict arises from scientific opinion not knowledge. This,
then, may be one way in which the *De iud. fac.* refines the argument
of the *Harm.*

47. *Harm.* Düring 5.24–6.11.

48. See *Harm*. Düring 1.5–6.

49. See *n*22.

50. Perhaps this is why Boethius qualifies the assertion with "as it were" (*quasi*) at *De inst. mus*. Friedlein 352.6.

51. Regarding Barker's remark, in *Greek Musical Writings* 163*n*5, that the "English cognate "criterion" is helpful in understanding this passage," see *n*19.

52. See *Harm*. Düring 3.14–20 and 3.20–4.7 respectively.

53. *De inst. mus*. Friedlein 352.15–17.

54. *De inst. mus*. Friedlein 352.17–26.

55. Boethius does, however, allow that hearing apprehends the truth in the trivial case, namely, the apprehension by hearing of the mere fact of a difference in pitch. See *De inst. mus*. Friedlein 353.18–20, 354.16–18. This case is trivial because, were it not so, there would be no subject of harmonic science. See Ptolemy *Harm*. Düring 4.10–13; also *n*35.

56. *De. inst. mus*. Friedlein 356.26–354.9.

57. The phrase *omne iudicium* does not mean "the entire judgment" [so Bower *Fundamentals of Music* 165] but "judgment as a whole."

58. *De inst. mus*. Friedlein 354.9–12; cf. Ptolemy *Harm*. Düring 3.19–20. Bower seems to read *labens* as "tottering" rather than "sliding, slipping away, escaping" at *De inst. mus*. Friedlein 352.17–26.

59. *De inst. mus*. Friedlein 354.13–25; cf. Ptolemy *Harm*. Düring 5.2–24.

60. *De inst. mus*. Friedlein 196.3–7; cf. Ptolemy *Harm*. Düring 5.13–19, 42.3–7.

61. We will not ask here what ontological status Boethius assigns to these whole number ratios and how he views their relation to number itself or to audible intervals.

62. *De inst. mus*. Friedlein 354.26–355.2; also 195.16–196.7. This is hardly what Ptolemy wrote in *Harm*. 1.2, but it is consistent with what Boethius has written previously in Book 5 as well as with what he proposes in *De inst. mus*. 1.9, a chapter in which he presents his own views and then elaborates them with reference to the Pythagoreans. It is noteworthy that Boethius' account of the Pythagoreans reveals the sort of theoretical stance that Ptolemy criticizes. See *Harm*. Düring 5.24–6.5.

63.   On Aristoxenus, see *De inst. mus.* Friedlein 355.2–5; on Ptolemy, 355.5–15.

64.   Bower does not capture the fact that *ut ne* here introduces a clause of *proviso.* See *Fundamentals of Music* 166.

65.   *De inst. mus.* 5.4, 5.8–9. Obviously, we do not agree with Bower that the critical difference between Ptolemy and the Pythagoreans concerns simply the measure of intervals. See *Fundamentals of Music* xxxvi. Nor do we follow Barker in supposing that Ptolemy presents himself as a member of the Pythagorean camp: Barker's argument consists in a listing of superficial similarities between the Ptolemaic and Pythagorean theories, and it ignores Ptolemy's *Almagest* and *De iud. fac.* See *Greek Musical Writings* 270–3.

66.   *De inst. arith.* 1.1. Boethius apparently coined the word *quadruvium*, later written as *quadrivium.* For an account of the role of this sort of pagan (Greek) learning up to the thirteenth century, see D. C. Lindberg "Science as Handmaiden: Roger Bacon and the Patristic Tradition" *Isis* (1987) 78:518–36.

67.   On Ptolemy's style in the *Harm.*, see R. P. Winnington-Ingram *Mode in Ancient Greek Music* (Cambridge 1936) 62, 67. Within a few centuries of Boethius, the Greek of Ptolemy and Euclid was, according to Rosenthal, "a dead language and known to be very different from the speech of contemporary Byzantines." See *The Classical Heritage* 16.

68.   It has also been argued that the last two theorems, which explicitly concern the *canon*, were added at a later time to the preceding nine. See P. Tannery "Inauthenticité de la « Division du canon » attribuée à Euclide" *Paul Tannery: Mémoires scientifiques* edd. J. L. Heiberg and H. G. Zeuthen 17 vols (Paris 1912–50) 3:213–5.

69.   A. C. Bowen "Euclid's *Sectio canonis* and the History of Pythagoreanism" *Science and Philosophy in Classical Greece* ed. Bowen ***Institute for Research in Classical Philosophy and Science: Sources and Studies in the History and Philosophy of Classical Science*** 2 (New York and London 1991) 164–87.

70.   The translations we offer do, however, incorporate our understanding of what the *Sectio canonis* is about. Readers interested in a fine translation that represents another view of the treatise should consult Barker "Methods and Aims in the Euclidean *Sectio canonis*" *Journal of Hellenic Studies* (1981) 101:1–16, and *Greek Musical Writings.* T. J. Mathiesen's version is so flawed, especially with respect

to Euclid's introduction, as to be unusable. See "An Annotated Translation of Euclid's Division of a Monochord" *Journal of Music Theory* (1975) 19:236–58. D. H. Fowler's translation of the introduction, *The Mathematics of Plato's Academy: A New Reconstruction* (Oxford 1987) 143–5, is derived from Barker.

71. Menge has Γ but B is required by the argument.

72. See, for example, ὁ Β πρὸς πὸν Δ in [2] Menge 160.9–10.

73. See Bowen "Euclid's *Sectio canonis* and Pythagoreanism." There is, of course, an obvious verbal difference between the Greek and Latin proofs: for there is no counterpart to Boethius' . . . *eius quod est* . . . (. . . of that which is . . .) because Greek unlike Latin has a definite article.

74. See, for example, Boethius' version of Euclid's third demonstration; Friedlein 303.19–22. Note that Boethius translates Euclid's διάστημα by *proportio*. Cf. Friedlein 303.21 and Menge 162.9. In general, both Euclid and Boethius apply to intervals truths that are stated in terms of ratios. See below for a discussion of what these ratios are ratios of.

75. As, for example, *De inst. mus.* Friedlein 303.6–10.

76. See *Sectio canonis* Menge 158.1–4 and *De inst. mus.* Friedlein 301.12–16, *Sectio canonis* Menge 158.4–16 and *De inst. mus.* Friedlein 301.17–23, and *Sectio canonis* Menge 158.16–24 and *De inst. mus.* Friedlein 301.23–27 respectively.

77. Compare *Sectio canonis* Menge 158.24–160.4 and *De inst. mus.* Friedlein 301.27–302.5.

78. See Friedlein 301.17–18; cf. Bower *Fundamentals of Music* 115.

79. See C. T. Lewis and C. Short edd. *A Latin Dictionary Founded on Andrews' Edition of Freund's Latin Dictionary* (Oxford 1879) 1909 col. 2.

80. *Sectio canonis* Menge 158.4–16.

81. Since the idea of frequency as the number of oscillatory motions *per* unit of time is much later than Euclid (or Boethius for that matter), the term πυκνότης, should be understood to designate only the *relative* numerosity or closeness-together of motions.

82. Friedlein 190.11–15.

83. See Menge 158.9–12: ἀναγκαῖον τοὺς μὲν ὀξυτέρους εἶναι, ἐπείπερ ἐκ πυκνοτέρων καὶ πλειόνων σύγκεινται κινήσεων, τοὺς δὲ

βαρυτέρους, ἐπείπερ ἐξ ἀραιοτέρων καὶ ἐλασσόνων σύγκεινται κινήσεων: "it is necessary that the former be higher in pitch because they
are composed of motions that are closer together and so more numerous
and that the latter be lower in pitch because they are composed of
motions that are less close together and so less numerous." See Bowen
"Euclid's *Sectio canonis* and Pythagoreanism" 168–73.

84. Compare Boethius *De inst. mus.* Friedlein 301.23–24 and Euclid *Sectio canonis* Menge 158.16–18.

85. This is consistent with what Boethius writes in *De inst. mus.*
2.20, of which the relevant lines are: "Thus, since concordance is the
established mixture of two notes, but (musical) sound is the occurrence
protracted at one pitch, of a melodic note; and since a (musical) sound
is the smallest particle of melody, and all sound depends on a striking
(*constet in pulsu*), and every striking arises from motion (*ex motu sit*);
and since some motions are equal and others are unequal. . . ." See
Friedlein 253.9–14.

In Bower's version, *omnis vero sonus constet in pulsu, pulsus vero
omnis ex motu* is rendered by "(since) all sound consists of pulsation,
and all pulsation of motion." See *Fundamentals of Music* 76. But
this is questionable on several counts. To begin, *pulsus* does not mean
"pulsation." For not only does it serve to translate πληγή (striking) in
De inst. mus. 4.1 when Boethius translates the introduction to Euclid's
Sectio canonis, but it also has this meaning in the present passage as
well as in *De inst. mus.* 1.14.

In this last passage, Boethius likens the propagation of sound in air
to the motion of the waves in a pool of water that has been disturbed by
a falling stone. Granted this might suggest to the unwary that Boethius
has grasped the fact that sound propagates as a three-dimensional oscillatory vibration of the medium, and perhaps this is what underlies
Bower's translating *pulsus* as "pulsation." Were it true of Boethius,
this would in itself be remarkable, since it is customary to place the
discovery of how sound propogates almost a millennium after him. To
demonstrate that the customary view is, in fact, correct lies beyond
the scope of this paper. (The reader may wish to consult Bowen "The
Foundations of Early Pythagorean Harmonic Science: Archytas, Fragment 1" *Ancient Philosophy* (1982) 2:79–104 on early Greek acoustical
theory.) For now, it suffices to draw attention to the fact that Boethius'
account is by no means unambiguously modern in its characterization
of sound. Indeed, what he writes in *De inst. mus.* 1.14 actually appears

to assume that the medium undergoes locomotion by a series of strikings: "thus, in this way when air that is struck (*pulsus*) makes a sound, it strikes (*pellit*—Bower's "affects," p. 21, obscures the point: *pulsus* is the perfect passive participle of *pello*) the other air nearby and sets in motion somehow a rounded wave of air, and the air is dispersed and strikes (*ferit*) at the same time the hearing of all those standing round." But in the wave-theory of sound transmission, the medium does not undergo locomotion.

Consequently, we doubt that *consto in pulsu* should be taken to mean "consists of pulsation" in *De inst. mus.* 2.20 Friedlein, 12–13, but prefer "depends on a striking" or even "comes in to existence on a striking"; similarly, we propose that motion is the source, and not a component, of a striking, and so prefer "arise from motion" for *ex motu sit* to Bower's "(consists) of motion." The advantage is that, in our account, the theory of sound in Books 1 and 2 of the *De inst. mus.* falls into line with that in Book 4—which means that Boethius is not committing a grievous error in Book 4 when he translates the introduction of Euclid's *Sectio canonis* in order to recapitulate the preceding books.

86. See Bowen "Euclid's *Sectio canonis* and Pythagoreanism."

87. For example, Barker "Methods and Aims in the Euclidean *Sectio canonis*" 158*n*9, *Greek Musical Writings* 190.

88. See Friedlein 301.7–12; also *n*84.

89. "Boethius and Nicomachus" 13.

90. See Barker "Methods and Aims in the Euclidean *Sectio canonis*," *Greek Musical Writings;* Barbera "Placing *Sectio canonis* in Historical and Philosophical Contexts" *Journal of Hellenic Studies* (1984) 104:157–61.

91. See A. C. Bowen "The Foundations of Early Pythagorean Harmonic Science" 2:79–104, "Euclid's *Sectio canonis* and Pythagoreanism" 183–7.

92. For a discussion of the claims made on the basis of Euclid's *Elements*, see W. R. Knorr "What Euclid Meant" *Science and Philosophy in Classical Greece* 119–63.

93. *In primum Euclidis elementorum librum commentarii* prol. ii ed. G. Friedlein *Procli Diadochi in primum Euclidis elementorum librum commentarii* (Leipzig 1873) 68.6–20. See T. L. Heath trans. *Euclid's Elements* 2d ed. (New York 1956) 1.1–2.

94. On Archimedes' supposed citation of Euclid, see E. J. Dijksterhuis *Archimedes* (Princeton 1987) 150n1. On the reference to the *Elements*, see Proclus *In primum Euclidis elementorum librum commentarii* prol. ii G. Friedlein ed. *Procli Diadochi in primum Euclidis elementorum librum commentarii* (Berlin 1873) 66.7–68.10. Archimedes *De sphæra et cylindro* edd. J. L. Heiberg and E. S. Stamatis *Archimedis opera omnia* 1 (Stuttgart 1972).

95. See A. C. Bowen and B. R. Goldstein "Hipparchus' Treatment of Early Greek Astronomy: The Case of Eudoxus and the Length of Daytime" *Proceedings of the American Philosophical Society* 43 (1991) 241–8.

96. *Euclidis phænomena* xxxii.

97. On the related question of the dates for Autolycus of Pitane, see Bowen and Goldstein "Hipparchus' Treatment of Early Greek Astronomy" 246n29.

98. On the idea of intellectual history in antiquity, see H. F. Cherniss "The History of Ideas and Ancient Greek Philosophy" *Studies in Intellectual History* (Baltimore 1953) 22–47; also *Harold Cherniss: Selected Papers* ed. L. Tarán (Leiden 1977) 36–61.

Previous Conference Publications